Walter Stephen was educated at schools and universities in Edinburgh and Glasgow, acquiring at an early age a love of travel and mild exploration. In his career as an educational advisor, he was able to pass on his love of Scotland and of the environment, among his achievements being the first successful Urban Studies Centre in Britain.

Retiring early, he has generated a stream of interesting and well-received books on Scottish themes, mainly, but also on such as Darwin, The War Poets Owen and Sassoon, the polymath Sir Patrick Geddes, Frank Fraser Darling (the first ecologist?) and *Willie Park Junior: The Man who took Golf to the World*.

His writing is warm, informative about so many people and places, sympathetic but never sentimental.

Walter Stephen

TWELVE GREAT SCOTS AND THEIR ROOTS

The Places Behind the Fame

AUSTIN MACAULEY PUBLISHERS™
LONDON * CAMBRIDGE * NEW YORK * SHARJAH

Copyright © Walter Stephen 2024

The right of Walter Stephen to be identified as author of this work has been asserted by the author in accordance with sections 77 and 78 of the Copyright, Designs and Patents Act 1988.

All rights reserved. No part of this publication may be reproduced, stored in a retrieval system, or transmitted in any form or by any means, electronic, mechanical, photocopying, recording, or otherwise, without the prior permission of the publishers.

Any person who commits any unauthorised act in relation to this publication may be liable to criminal prosecution and civil claims for damages.

The story, experiences, and words are the author's alone.

A CIP catalogue record for this title is available from the British Library.

ISBN 9781035821259 (Paperback)
ISBN 9781035821266 (ePub e-book)

www.austinmacauley.com

First Published 2024
Austin Macauley Publishers Ltd®
1 Canada Square
Canary Wharf
London
E14 5AA

JUST AS IT IS BETTER to travel hopefully than to arrive so the main pleasures in a quest are often the serendipitous meetings on the way to the goal.

A book like this demands a lot of poking about in a medley of places and the picking of the brains of a variety of people. I have benefitted from meeting a galaxy of often bemused but always helpful interviewees, most of whom did not give their names.

Of the known contributors, Ian Campbell, the second-last native Gaelic speaker in Strontian, added living flesh to academic bones. For Rhynie, Bill Eddie of Edinburgh University provided the initial impetus, while Colin and Amanda Reid put Rhynie's past into a modern context. Anne Murray of Rhynie Woman, a vigorous local ginger group, provided Figs 13 and 14. Gratefully acknowledged. Kenneth MacLean of Perth, as ever, filled in gaps authoritatively. Richard McKendrick of the Inchnadamph Hotel does much more than feed and water those who follow the exploits of Peach and Horne, and has provided the evidence for their work in Fig 8. Gratefully acknowledged. Alex Geddes, from Auckland, New Zealand has provided Fig 18 from the Geddes family collection. Again, gratefully acknowledged.

The staff of the great national institutions, and some other organisations, have, as ever, supported the project with extreme competence and have gone beyond this with enthusiastic interest. Historic Environment Scotland opened their files and provided Fig 16. Gratefully acknowledged. The Map Library of the National Library of Scotland has once again backed my efforts. The Royal Museum of Scotland opened my eyes and enabled Fig 14. Gratefully acknowledged. Aberdeenshire Council has given a safe home to Rhynie Man, accessible to all, in office hours, for which we must all be grateful. The National Trust for

Scotland gave access to Thrums. The British Geological Society has generously permitted publication of Fig 7. Gratefully acknowledged. Scottish Sculpture Workshop helped to conceptualise the meanings of stones in their landscape.

Twinkl Educational Publishing provided the base map for Fig 1. Gratefully acknowledged. Ian Grahame, my admirable and esteemed former colleague, has once again ironed out my difficulties with the new technology. My late brother, Olrig, who loved all Scottish places, provided the sketches which feature here as Figs 2, 3, 4 and 5. Sadly, he is no longer with us to enjoy the rest of the book, which he would have done.

Introduction

In 2011, Luath Press published my *Walter's Wiggles: The Random Thoughts of a Random Traveller*—in effect, fifteen essays examining the nature of Place. The Place, Walter's Wiggles, in Zion National Park, Utah, is more than an adventurous climb, it is a metaphor for life.

From Refrigerator Canyon, Walter's Wiggles are a series of spectacular traverses leading to Scout Lookout and Angels Landing (we are in Mormon territory here). The park guide says:
Strenuous. Long drop-offs and narrow trails. Not for anyone fearful of heights. Last 0.5 mile follows a steep narrow ridge; chains have been added for safety.

There we have it, but what the guide does not mention is that, in late afternoon thunderstorms, the chains make excellent lightning conductors!

Just as in *Pilgrim's Progress,* the traveller starts in the damp dark slough and toils up the endless traverses to emerge in the bright sunlight, nearer to God and salvation.

Twelve Great Scots is not a straightforward sequel to *Walter's Wiggles*. The main preoccupation is still Place, but the places are not chosen at random, being associated with Great Scots. The triangulation is complete with an examination of the nature of each one's Fame. A feature of the book is that description is given a practical element—and a challenge—by each chapter being given a Trail, so that the reader can check the veracity of the author's descriptions and analysis.

Great Scott! (with two 't's) is said to be an interjection of surprise, amazement, or dismay. It is, or was, a distinctive but inoffensive exclamation, popular in the second half of the 19th century and the early 20th century. The 2010 edition of the *Oxford Dictionary of English* labels the expression as 'dated' and simply identifies it as an 'arbitrary euphemism for *Great God!*' Where did the term come from? As early as 1830, Sir Walter Scott was being referred to in an Australian poem as 'the great Scott'. Another poem of 1871, celebrating the centenary of Scott's birth, almost anticipates *Flower of Scotland*:

Whose wild free charms,
he chanted forth Great Scott!
When shall we see
thy like again? Great Scott!

Mark Twain disdained Scott. In *A Connecticut Yankee in King Arthur's Court* (1889), the main character repeatedly utters 'great Scott' as an oath, and in *The Adventures of Huckleberry Finn* (1884), he names a sinking boat the *Walter Scott*.

Great Scot, as a descriptive phrase, has been around for quite some time and was particularly popular around 1900, when there was a definite atmosphere of national consciousness, verging on mild nationalism, in Scotland.

Monuments to Wallace and other Great Scots, usually in Scottish Baronial style, were springing up in 'a' the airts'. Great Scots abounded. Keir Hardie's Scottish Labour Party merged with the Independent Labour Party to give a particularly Scottish flavour to left wing politics in Scotland. RG Cunninghame Graham was an aristocratic Liberal who was twice a founder member, Socialist and Nationalist.

As Professor Smout says: 'It is not given to many to found two opposed political parties in their lifetime'. If becoming prime minister is a measure of greatness, Great Scots were there too.

Andrew Carnegie was a Great Scot whose greatness lay in his reluctance to die rich and in his generous use of his wealth to uplift his fellow Scots through education. Yet, he left Scotland at an early age to make his fortune in the United States. Dozens of engineers, inventors and entrepreneurs could have been described as Great Scots.

In this book, twelve Great Scots and the places they are associated with are examined. But what makes a Great Scot? What is greatness? Malvolio in Shakespeare's *Twelfth Night,* a pompous twit if ever there was one, opines: 'Some are born great, some acquire greatness, and some have greatness thrust upon them'. None of my Great Scots was born great. There is no Robert, the Bruce here, no Mary, Queen of Scots.

There are four knights in my list, but they all came from modest beginnings, and made their way up the greasy pole by native genius and hard work. While none of them died in poverty, only two of them, a professional tennis player and an author and playwright, could be described as wealthy.

For some, their greatness might seem very mundane. Both James Hutton and Dr Mackie of Elgin looked at the stones in the drystane dykes that were a familiar part of the Scottish landscape, and came up with ideas that revolutionised the way we look at the very fundamental origins of the earth and the very first plants and animals to emerge from the sea. Their greatness lay in their ability to see their world with fresh eyes and to convince the world of the new truths they had discovered.

Dr Jim Swire lost his daughter in the Lockerbie disaster, and found greatness thrust upon him when he found himself almost alone in fighting for truth and justice in the face of international intrigue and corruption.

Leaving greatness aside for the moment, what is a Scot? At the time of the 2014 Referendum on Scottish independence, there was great discussion as to who should be entitled to vote. Anglo-Scots and third generation members of Caledonian Societies around the globe thought they must be entitled to vote, because they were interested in Scotland and Scottish life.

The Bruces were Normans who had lands in England as well as in Scotland. For these, they had done homage to the English king and had sworn loyalty to him. And now we have a distinguished professor suggesting that 'Good King Robert' was not born in Turnberry Castle but 'almost certainly in Essex' in the village of Writtle, near Chelmsford. So, was our Hero-King really Essex Man? A very different kettle of fish! Quite unthinkable!

Mary Stuart was born in Linlithgow and became Queen of Scotland six days later. For her own safety, she was taken over to France at the age of 5. She was brought up in the French court where she was, for one year, Queen of France. As a young widow of nineteen, she came back to Scotland with a train of French courtiers and adventurers.

She claimed the throne of England and spent the last eighteen years of her life in custody there. How Scottish could Mary, Queen of Scots, have been?

As a useful parallel, I have taken the English game of cricket. For many years, first-class cricket was organised around the County Championship.

In the twenty-one interwar years, from 1919 to 1939, Yorkshire were County Champions twelve times, followed by Lancashire (five times). The 'wooden spoon' was collected by Northamptonshire eight times, by Worcestershire five times, and by Glamorgan twice. It was clear that there were vast disparities between counties, particularly between the big industrial counties and the smaller ones.

Qualification for a county was based on birthplace, and cricket lore is full of stories of expectant mothers being driven madly through the night so that the son could be born within a county—usually Yorkshire. Something had to be done to contrive a more even—and more genuinely competitive—competition.

The answer was residential qualification. People could play for Yorkshire, for example, if they had been born in the county. But a Yorkshireman could qualify for another county by residing in that county, say Somerset, for two years, playing in League cricket and non-championship matches for a living.

This helped to even things up a bit, but not enough, so Special Registration was brought in. A weak county, like Somerset or Northamptonshire, with specific needs, could apply for certain individuals to be specially registered by the MCC to play immediately.

As a result, around 1950, the batting line-up of Northamptonshire regularly looked like this:

Brookes (Yorkshire)
Oldfield (Lancashire)
Livingston (Australia)
Jakeman (Yorkshire)*
Broderick (Lancashire)
Tribe (Australia)
Brown (Surrey)*
* = Special Registration

For the so-called amateurs, things were easier. Freddie Brown was an amateur who played for Surrey and England. In 1949, he was given a job with an engineering firm in Northampton and appointed captain of Northants, as preparation for the England captaincy, which he did fifteen times.

When we consider what makes a Scot, the cricketing experience is quite helpful. Self-evidently, anyone born in Scotland must be a Scot, whether they like it or not. I am not aware of anyone hurtling north along the M6 (like the eloping couples in the 19th century) in order to register as a Scottish birth.

People who choose to make their lives in Scotland can be seen as acquiring a residential qualification, while someone like Dr Jim Swire, who chose to take on the forces of the establishment when there was no local fighter on hand, could be seen as being under special registration.

As a geographer, my first question is always 'Where?' And my second is 'Why there?'. Place is the stock in trade of the geographer, and for each Great Scot, I have a Place. In fact, this book could be thought of as a Celebration of Place, as well as of personalities.

How does one acquire a sense of Place? I can only explain through personal experience. One of my earliest memories is of the last summer before World War 2, when my father, my mother and I toured Scotland in a Baby Austin Seven, wild camping. My father was probably inspired by HV Morton's *In Search of Scotland* of 1929, in which the authoritative journalist, who had scooped the opening of the tomb of Tutankhamun in 1923, toured Scotland in a bull-nosed Morris.

(*In Search of Scotland Again* followed in 1933, and *The Splendour of Scotland* in 1976).

As a good journalist, Morton was able to dissect out from the Statistical Accounts the facts and legends of the past, and enliven them with his experiences on the road. In his time, he was very influential, and one can still detect traces of his writing in much later Scottish travel books.

My father and I were on the first bus tour to the Highlands after the war. Suilven, the 'pillar-mountain' of the Norsemen, particularly haunted me and was a magnet for many cycle explorations, using the youth hostels—cheap, with good companionship and a great diversity of location and buildings—from a collection of wooden huts in Glen Affric, miles from any road, to the 20th century Carbisdale Castle, with 250 beds and a splendid hall full of sculptures.

Every summer, our family, now numbering five, would set off for a Grand Tour of Scotland, using the hostels. Alasdair Alpin MacGregor's many books gave us information and structure. Although, some parts now seem embarrassingly sentimental, in those days they took us into unusual corners. They could be highly amusing and, for me, opened up the geological wonders and challenges of the northwest.

By now, there was a steady stream of interesting information coming through with a growing national consciousness. Books like ARB Haldane's *The Drove Roads of Scotland* (1952) and *New Ways through the Glens* (1962), and Sandy Fenton's *Scottish Country Life* (1976), demonstrated that there was more to Scotland than Mary, Queen of Scots, and Bonnie Prince Charlie. The superb Collins *New Naturalist* series sorted out the environment—climate, vegetation and soils.

Frank Fraser Darling contributed *Natural History in the Highlands and Islands* (1947) and led the work, which led to *West Highland Survey* (1956). AG Williamson, in *Twixt Forth and Clyde* (1946), took the devastated mining and industrial landscape of Central Scotland, a veritable hell of mines, mills and polluted streams, and showed us how interesting it was, once the surface layers had been peeled off.

A very popular format for the travel book is *Travelling in So-and-so's Footsteps,* taking an early traveller's account and following it today, noting what has changed and what has not. William and Dorothy Wordsworth were joined by Samuel Taylor Coleridge in a tour of Scotland in the late summer of 1803, a tour which inspired some of Wordsworth's best writing. At Arrochar, Coleridge 'broke away', giving rise to Carol Kyros Walker's *Breaking Away: Coleridge in Scotland* (2002), with notes, letters and descriptions.

A former colleague, Stuart Campbell, has given us an excellent new slant on this format in *Boswell's Bus Pass* (2006). Dr Johnson and James Boswell toured the Highlands and Islands in 1773, resulting in, respectively, *Journey to the Western Islands of Scotland* (1775) and *Journal of a Tour to the Hebrides* (1785). For both this was quite an adventure, as the Highlands were still a problematical region at that time, and Johnson was quite an elderly gentleman of 64.

Johnson grudged the expense of bringing with him Francis Barber, his black servant, but Boswell took his 'man', Joseph Ritter, 'a Bohemian, a fine stately fellow above six feet high' who spoke many languages and reported back to Boswell's wife in Edinburgh. So we have three accounts—one fictional—of what happened on Johnson's Highland jaunt.

Campbell chooses to follow in their tracks, more or less, using his recently acquired bus pass, which gives him the opportunity to comment on local people and the elderly, in particular, as well as straightforwardly reporting on then and now. As befits a former adviser in English, Campbell's style is clever, clear and irreverent, although the last quality wears a little thin near the end. For the purist, there may be a little concern at the blurring between truth, the experience of the historic pair, and the modern mélange of narrative and comment, but, all in all, this is an excellent travel book in the modern style.

A further twist to the format was given by Mairi Hedderwick in 1992 with her *Highland Journey: A Sketching Tour of Scotland retracing the footsteps of Victorian artist John T Reid*. This is multi-dimensional, switching between Reid's journal entries and Hedderwick's narrative and comments, and between

Reid's engravings and Hedderwick's free sketches. Sometimes they are paired, as with the stones at Callanish, where Hedderwick has added a note, drawing our attention that 'Big stone to left missing'. Thus, her book is a record of change as well as a straightforward narrative.

Ross Noble, in 2003, in his *North and West: Exploring the North and West Highlands and Islands of Scotland,* alternates chapters in the prehistory and history of the Highlands and Islands with reminiscences of 'explorations'. His book begins with *The Walk to Ardvar*, in July 1961, and ends with *The Walk to Ardvar*, March 1996.

Twelve Great Scots and their Roots: The Places behind the Fame is my contribution to this moving staircase of the interpretation of Scotland, the Scots, and their environment. Quite simply, it takes twelve Scots, each with a claim to fame, and relates each to a place in Scotland, which may be the root of their fame. For each place, there is an illustrated description and an explanation of why its name has (or has not!) resonated around the world, and with whom.

In case any reader is unconvinced by my arguments, each description is followed by a guide or trail so that the reader can, if interested, cover the territory, see for themselves and check my veracity.

I must emphasise the importance of the trails. They are not put in just to fill out the text. They are meant to supplement the overall narrative by giving detailed information at particular locations. Fig 1 gives the names and locations of twelve places associated with my Great Scots. Imagine the reactions. Where is Edinburgh? What about St Andrews? Loch Lomond?

Currently, Edinburgh buses carry an advertisement for 'HMS Britannia—Scotland's Best Visitor Attraction'. Surely Leith should be on the map! Why don't you get a life?

My Places are not competing with these, and other, very worthy and well worth visiting places. No statistics of footfall are available for them. For only one is there any admission charge. Hardly a café or gift shop is to be found among them. Amazingly, many of the residents of some of these places are unaware of their celebrity. Some are scarcely visible on the map.

Looking at Plate 3, one sees a cluster of enthusiasts who have made the journey all the way from Wyoming in order to see for themselves at Inchnadamph. What? And why? They then proceeded to another, even more isolated, place in Berwickshire, Siccar Point. Why? Because that was the location of one of the most important discoveries in the history of the world's creation; a discovery which turned scientific thinking about time upside down.

The first question a geographer always asks is 'Where?' And the second is 'Why there?' Fig 1 gives twelve simple answers to Where? but Why there? provokes even more questions.

What has number 38 in the Periodic Table of Elements to do with a little Highland village? What is a thrum? And why can we not find Thrums on a published map? What do a great Canadian city and an obscure hamlet in Mull have in common? Why is it pointless to go looking for evidence of the first creatures to make it on to the land?

How can we leave behind the traumas of a childhood massacre? Will we ever get the truthful answer to the Lockerbie question?

Familiar or not, we have twelve interesting places with twelve interesting—and sometimes unlikely—stories behind them. And now, in order to set the scene and get the reader thinking before embarking on Chapter One, we have some Quotable Quotes from the famous and not-so-famous.

Fig 1: Weel-kent Places
(Base map—Twinkl Educational Publishing)

Some Quotable Quotes

But be not afraid of greatness: some men are born great, some achieve greatness, and some have greatness thrust upon them.
William Shakespeare (Playwright) (1564-1616)

I never saw a country that seemed so torn and convulsed.
Thomas Pennant (Traveller/mapmaker) (1726-1798)

My lady, there are few more impressive sights in the world than a Scotsman on the make.
JM Barrie (Writer) (1860-1937)

The mind seemed to grow giddy by looking so far into the abyss of time...we became sensible how much further reason may sometimes go than imagination may venture to follow.
John Playfair (Natural Philosophy professor) (1748-1819)

The result...of our present enquiry is that we find no vestige of a beginning, no prospect of an end.
James Hutton (Geologist) (1726-97)

Another aspect of Hutton's greatness was revealed in 2003. Every May, Christian Aid have an enormous book sale in St Andrew's Church in Edinburgh's New Town. James Hutton's *Theory of the Earth*, in its first edition of 1795, raised £5,000, the record sum raised for anything at the Sale in its first fifteen years.

'Behold the Tiber', the vain Roman cried,
Viewing the ample Tay from Baiglie's side;
But where's the Scot that would the vaunt repay,
And hail the puny Tiber for the mighty Tay!
                              Sir Walter Scott (Writer) (1771-1832)

Sometimes the Beautiful is more useful than the Useful.
                              Patrick Geddes (Polymath) (1854-1932)

So beyond working and playing comes remembering, in some ways the happiest of all.
                              Patrick Geddes (Polymath) (1854-1932)

Every Victorian worth his or her aesthetic salt could turn off a neat watercolour or two before tea.
                              Mairi Hedderwick (Writer/artist) (1939-)

From Scenes like these, old Scotia's grandeur springs,
That makes her lov'd at home, rever'd abroad:
Princes and lords are but the breath of kings,
'An honest man's the noble work of God'.
                              Robert Burns (Poet) (1759-1796)

Schiehallion! Schiehallion! Schiehallion!
                              Edwin Morgan (Poet) (1920-2010)

Chapter One

Where the Mind Grows Giddy
James Hutton and Siccar Point

Siccar Point is on the cliff-bound coast of Berwickshire. In 1788, three gentlemen of the Scottish Enlightenment sailed from Dunglass round the coast to Siccar Point in search of enlightenment. Sir James Hall of Dunglass (1761-1832) was the first to demonstrate experimentally how limestone was metamorphosed into marble. John Playfair, professor of Natural Philosophy at Edinburgh (1748-1819), wrote up the jaunt in 1805.

Playfair and Hall were fine fellows and have their monuments, but James Hutton was a Great Scot whose name still resounds around the world.

Hutton (1726-1797) was almost a stereotype of the Enlightenment Scot. Born in Edinburgh, he attended the Royal High School, had three years at Edinburgh University, moved on to the University of Paris and took the degree of Doctor of Medicine at Leiden in the Netherlands, with a thesis on the circulation of the blood.

He returned to Edinburgh to take up the practical applications of chemistry, do some experimental work on dyes, and run a business manufacturing salt for use in industry.

His father having left him two farms in Berwickshire, Hutton became an agricultural improver and an exemplar of the Agricultural Revolution. Field drainage gave him an interest in stones, their composition and appearance. Around 1768, he began to immerse himself in geological fieldwork and systematically covered Glen Tilt in Perthshire, the island of Arran, the borders and in and around Edinburgh.

All this time, he had been brooding about the Earth and its formation, resulting, in 1795, in the publication of his findings in *Theory of the Earth, with Proofs and Illustrations.* His suggestions (with proofs!) that the Earth had a molten iron core and, more importantly, was immeasurably old and was certainly not created in six days, blew apart the worlds of science and religion. The dust has still not quite settled.

Hutton was a quiet man who did not seek controversy. His portrait, by a young Henry Raeburn, hangs in the Scottish National Portrait Gallery and shows a prim buttoned-up man, which he certainly was not. Malcolm Rider says: 'The picture by Raeburn is awful...The picture looks even worse in the original...than it does in small reproductions.'

Robert Louis Stevenson's comment was: '...looking altogether trim and narrow, as if he cared more about fossils than young ladies.'

Edinburgh at the time was famous, or notorious, for its (all-male) clubs with rituals and heavy drinking. (I know of two which are still in existence, the Cape Club with its Gentlemen of the Cape and the Crochallan Fencibles, whose most famous member was Robert Burns).

Hutton was a member of the Oyster Club—literary figures devoted to the eating of oysters while they discussed topical matters. Hutton and his friend, Joseph Black (discoverer of magnesium, latent heat, specific heat and carbon dioxide), were delegated to find new premises for their meetings. They found a very suitable place with 'a whole bevy of well-dressed but somewhat brazen-faced young ladies'. It was a house of ill-repute! History does not tell us what happened next.

Hutton never married, but had one illegitimate son.

This was the man who led the little expedition, and in one of the finest descriptive passages in the language, Playfair wrote:

On landing at this point, we found that we actually trod on the primeval rock...Dr Hutton was highly pleased with appearances that set in so clear a light the different foundations of the parts which compose the exterior crust of the earth and proceeded to interpret the 'palpable evidence' that lay before them. Playfair was clearly moved by the processes revealed to him so clearly.

We often said to ourselves, What clearer evidence could we have had of the different formation of these rocks, and of the long interval which separated their formation, had we actually seen them emerging from the bosom of the deep?

We felt ourselves carried back to the time when the schistus was still at the bottom of the sea...

An epoch still more remote presented itself...

Revolutions still more remote appeared in the distance of this extraordinary Perspective.

The mind seemed to grow giddy by looking so far into the abyss of time.
(Author's italics)

What had Hutton seen and explained which had so disturbed his fellow-travellers and which was to change everyone's notion of how and when the world was formed?

Had we been there he would have pointed out to us shales and other rocks laid down under water in Silurian times, over many years. (PLATE 1a) and (Fig 2)

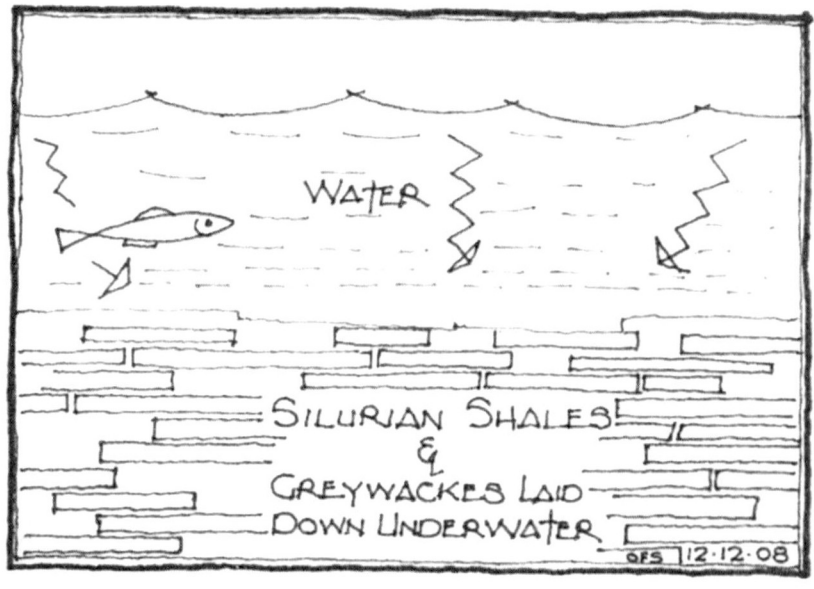

Fig 2: Siccar Point, Phase 1
(Olrig Stephen)

These rocks were then tilted, uplifted and partially worn away by wind and water over an immense period of time. (Fig 3)

Fig 3: Siccar Point, Phase 2 (Olrig Stephen)

In the Old Red Sandstone period, the Silurian rocks were covered by water and more sediments were laid down, including sandstones and a rock like sandstone, which contained fragments from the Silurian rocks. Again, a great deal of time was required for this to happen. (Fig 4)

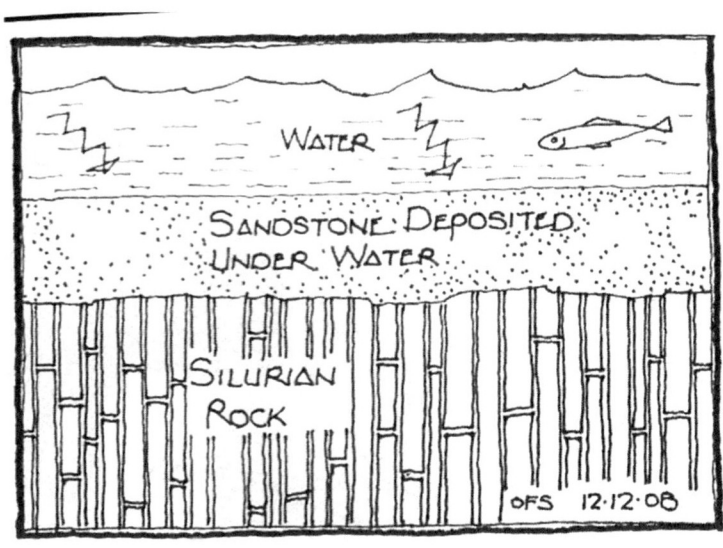

Fig 4: Siccar Point, Phase 3
(Olrig Stephen)

The whole mass was lifted and slightly tilted. The line separating the old rocks from the new rocks is called an unconformity, and symbolises a very long time in which rocks were uplifted and eroded, then submerged and covered up. (Fig 5)

I find it very helpful to note what I call 'an urban unconformity' (see Fig 6). On the left in this street in the Roseburn area of Edinburgh is a typical tenement block of the 1890s, four storeys in height, stone-built, with minimal front gardens and a forest of chimneys. On the right is a block clearly influenced by the Garden City movement, dating from the 1920s. There are gardens front and rear. The houses are lower, have big bay windows and are of stone-fronted or harled brick.

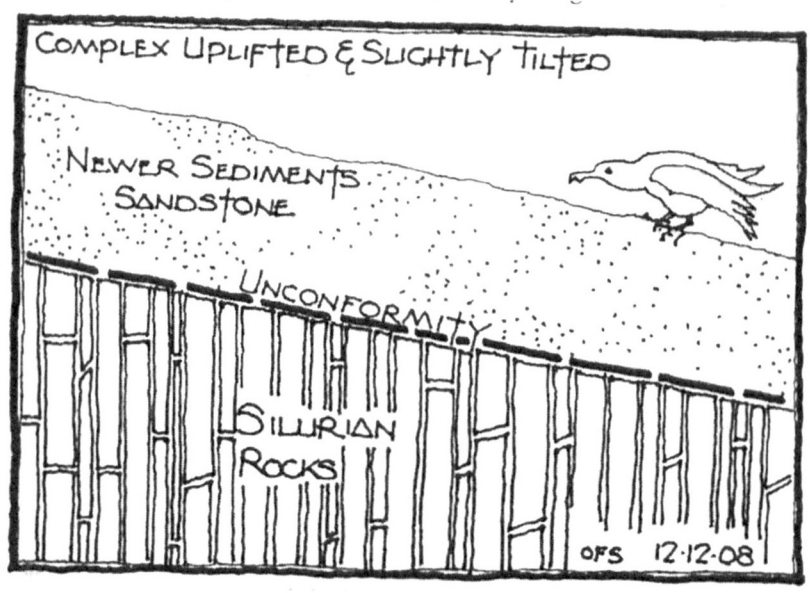

Fig 5: Siccar Point, Phase 4
(Olrig Stephen)

Fig 6: An Urban Unconformity

The tenement block was the last to be built in the street, while the villas were the first to be built when house-building resumed in the 1920s. The sharp division between them is the urban unconformity and represents thirty years of inactivity in house-building in Edinburgh, but of quite dramatic change in other parts of the world, notably in the period 1914-18.

About fifty years ago, it used to give me great pleasure, away in the far north-west, to stand with my left foot on the Torridonian sandstone, laid down before there was life on earth—and my right on the Cambrian quartzite—when there was an explosion of life. I would point to the junction and invite speculation as to what may have happened in the millions of years represented by that line. (We now know there were some traces of life in the Torridonian—but the staggering contrast still remains.)

Playfair's summing up of the day was that: 'How much further reason may sometimes go than imagination can venture to follow'. Hutton's Unconformity is no bigger than a decent-sized living-room, yet its message is clear. Although, there were rumblings of discontent in the scientific community at the biblical account of Creation, it was the evidence from Siccar Point and dozens of other localities and Hutton's *Theory of the Earth* (1795) which convinced the world of the great age of our planet.

In a monumental phrase, he summed up the concept of 'deep time': 'we find no vestige of a beginning, no prospect of an end'.

He also made it clear that there was no need to invoke catastrophic or miraculous intervention to create a landscape. The processes working on land and sea today are the same as worked in the past: 'The present is the key to the past'.

Hutton is often described as 'The Father of Geology'. From Siccar Point, he took 'one giant stride' in the search for truth about where we live. Others followed. In 1859, Charles Darwin published *The Origin of Species,* and in 1882, Walther Flemming discovered what we now call chromosomes. In 1900, Mendel's work on heredity was rediscovered.

Alfred Wegener's hypothesis of Continental Drift of 1910 evolved into plate tectonics, which from the 1960s, answered many of our basic questions about the earth's structure and history.

Not exactly a shrine, Siccar Point is known all over the world and is, in fact, a very suitable place for pilgrimage (but not for the disabled!). Great sheets of Old Red Sandstone conglomerate are worked over by the North Sea at high tide. One's only living companions are the shags drying off on the rocks and a few busy waders. It is just oneself and the rocks, and one's thoughts.

Like Hutton, we can 'grow giddy by looking so far into the abyss of time'.

The Trail

The visitor from the south, eager to follow in the steps of Hutton, could easily follow the A1 from Berwick, 'do' Siccar Point and go back home. A better option would be to follow the A68 over the border to Jedburgh and then on to Edinburgh, mopping-up the Edinburgh locations before finishing off with the real thing at Siccar Point. This route is described below.

1. **Allars Mill, Jedburgh**. Coming in to Jedburgh from the south, just before the Abbey Bridge, turn left into a large car park on a demolished mill site (Allars Mill). Across the Jed is the ruined Jedburgh Abbey.

Since I was here last, the river cliff upstream on the far bank has been covered by vegetation. An information board tells us that Hutton's Unconformity is not accessible as it is on private land. However, the near bank has been made into a park, and in it is an excellent sculpture by Max Nowell.

Whatever its aesthetic merits, it brilliantly captures the spirit of the unconformity, with the verticality of the base contrasting with the colour and horizontality of the 'newer' rock and the absolutely clear line of division (unconformity) between them. (PLATE 1b). On one of the seats nearby are said to be the closing words from *Theory of the Earth.*

One would expect a point on the trail to be the **Scottish National Portrait Gallery**, where there is a portrait of James Hutton by the young Henry Raeburn. It shows a prim, buttoned-up man—which Hutton was certainly not.

Malcolm Rider says: 'The picture by Raeburn is awful…The picture looks even worse in the original…than it does in small reproductions.'

Robert Louis Stevenson's comment was '…looking altogether trim and narrow, as if he cared more about fossils than young ladies.'

It is not recommended as part of the Trail, but there is another representation of Hutton in the Portrait Gallery which is worth a glance, if only to note the company Hutton keeps. High up on the north side of the atrium of the Gallery is a portrait of Caledonia, around whom is a great frieze of Famous Scots, arranged chronologically.

Shyly tucked in between and behind Burns and Telford, those other giants of the time, is James Hutton, looking quite aquiline. Nearby are the giants of the next generation—Sir Charles Lyell and Sir Roderick Murchison.

2. **St John's Hill** is off Holyrood Road in Edinburgh. The **Hutton Memorial Garden** was created in 1997 on the site of 3 St John's Hill, where Hutton lived from 1770 and wrote his epoch-making *The Theory of the Earth.* The location is authentic but unprepossessing, being surrounded by monolithic car parks, university buildings and tired public housing.

The garden is littered with empty cans but no longer seems to be a refuge for the homeless. But 'I to the hills will lift mine eyes' and between the blocks is the inspiration of Salisbury Crags, which Hutton must have experienced every morning.

Around the garden are granite, gneiss, conglomerate and sandstone boulders from Glen Tilt, Arran and other places associated with Hutton. A large block of

Triassic sandstone carries a memorial plaque with a cartoon from Kay's *Edinburgh Portraits,* showing the elongated philosopher with his geological hammer attacking a cliff face of weel-kent Edinburgh characters. The plaque reads:

James Hutton
MD FRSE
Philosopher and Scientist
Founder of Modern Geology
'We find no vestige of a beginning
No prospect of an end'

There is also a little plaque which reads: 'This plaque is non-metallic and has no scrap or resale value', and tells you something about the area.

Although, Our Dynamic Earth is only five minutes away, logic demands that we now make our way into Holyrood Park where we find, at the south end of Salisbury Crags:

3. **Hutton's Section**, marked with an interpretation board. An exposure about 25 metres long has been closely examined for over two centuries. (PLATE 2a)

What is there to see? Sedimentary rocks—red and white Upper Old Red Sandstone—dip to the east at about 20 degrees, parallel to the Salisbury Crags sill above. Above these is a mass of basalt, which has clearly behaved as a liquid, breaking through the sandstone layers. At one point, near the right-hand end, the molten basalt has flowed under a sandstone block and almost prised it loose. At the other end of the section, the basalt has broken through, crumpling the sediments.

A thin gap can be seen where the two rocks meet. This was filled with black volcanic glass (obsidian) where the magma cooled swiftly, but the evidence has been 'eroded' by souvenir hunters and scientific looters. In the basalt, the crystal size increases upwards as the molten rock took longer to cool. Conversely, the sandstone sediments are baked more near the line of contact with the basalt.

The basalt is more resistant to erosion than the sandstone, so that it stands out from it. Which takes us 100 metres along the Radical Road to:

4. **Hutton's Rock**, which stands 2-3 metres high in the largest of the old quarries. The tradition is that the quarrymen preserved the Rock at Hutton's request. Incredible though it may seem today, in the early 19th century, Salisbury Crags were being furiously quarried away and sold to pave the streets of London. As Lord Cockburn, an early conservationist, wrote in *Memorials of His Time* (1856):

This would have implied the obliteration of some of the strata which all Edinburgh ought to have revered as Hutton's local evidence of the Theory of the Earth, and one of the most peculiar features of our scenery.

The guilty would have been—first the Hereditary Keeper of the Park (the Earl of Haddington) who made money of the devastation by selling the stones; secondly, the Town Council and the Road Trustees, who bought them; thirdly, the Crown and its local officers, who did not check the atrocity. Of these, the Crown was the least criminal.

Hutton's Rock is a good example of differential erosion. It is made of teschenite (a coarse-grained basalt) through which runs a vein of impure haematite (iron oxide), which is visibly disintegrating more rapidly than the teschenite.

The view from here is superb, with Edinburgh's many hills, remnants of vulcanism, and the Lammermuirs, many miles to the south, marking the Southern Uplands Boundary Fault. Down below note Our Dynamic Earth, which is our next stop.

5. **Our Dynamic Earth** is the only visitor centre in the UK dedicated to telling the life story of Planet Earth and was Scotland's main permanent contribution to the Millennium celebrations.

Edinburgh had a huge planning problem when the Holyrood breweries pulled out. The solution has been the new Parliament building, a newspaper office, hotels, chi-chi housing and Our Dynamic Earth, a giant marquee grafted on to the sandstone foundations of a former brewery.

Approached from Holyrood Road on the north, Our Dynamic Earth is in two parts. First is a large saucer-shaped theatre, into and round which drive buses and cars. On the slopes are, quite literally, Rock Gardens, a Geo Garden, Scotland's

Journey and five Slices Through Scotland, all illustrated with massive rock samples.

In the centre, one descends into Earth's Core, with a variety of media fostering interest in the riches still to come. Notable is a cartoon rock opera in which Hutton and Jameson, another Edinburgh man, slug it out! And all this is free!

The main centre is not free; how could it be with its superlative use of all the media and an abundance of eager young interpreters? One descends and enters an imaginative reconstruction of James Hutton's library, where the great man (or a hologram) tells us about Siccar Point and what stemmed from it, engaging in conversation with other Edinburgh figures like Lyell, Darwin, Peach and Horne, even Arthur Holmes—under whom the author studied!

The centre is really a succession of theatres and, while we are waiting for the Time Machine, we circle round a large globe slowly rotating and changing to illustrate plate tectonics, with the plates, earthquake and volcanic zones. The mind grew giddy at Siccar Point in 1788, and coming out of the Time Machine one is also giddy, having been besieged by untold millions and billions.

(Children are a main target for the organisers—they are addressed 'Hallo, small life forms'—and I was impressed by some of the parents). Next, we were inside a volcano, with glowing lava and the sudden cracking noise and wobbly floor of an earthquake.

The Work of the Ice had much that was recognisably Scottish, and we then moved into Life on Earth, which was spacious, very varied and had dozens of hands-on activities. Then we had a succession of environments, the oceans, the polar regions, the rainforests, beautifully presented but also bringing in the difficult question of how Man, who is now so powerful, is to relate to his Dynamic Earth.

Our Dynamic Earth superbly deals with the origins and development of our planet. It does not set out to entertain, but it uses the technology of entertainment to engage and inform. It is not a James Hutton Heritage Centre, but it clearly sets out the line of succession from his *Theory of the Earth* and his practical demonstrations.

6. After the hi-tech of Our Dynamic Earth **Siccar Point,** the real thing, may seem an anti-climax. To get there, leave Edinburgh by the A1. After 55Km (35 miles), just beyond Cockburnspath, at the beginning of a dual carriageway turn left (north) down the A1107. Go over the railway bridge, then the fine viaduct over the gorge of the Pease Burn and turn left on the road signposted to Pease Bay, also with a sign advertising Drysdales' vegetable-processing plant 'growing great vegetables in the fertile lowlands of Scotia'.

Continue downhill till the road begins to loop sharply to the left. Go straight ahead, through sandstone gateposts with another Drysdales' sign. After about a mile, partly following a glacial meltwater channel, you will arrive at Siccar Point Visitors Car Park, 'developed and maintained by Drysdales'.

(Just ahead is the large processing plant. There is a potential conflict between those who want to keep Siccar Point inviolate and the desire of the vegetable processors to expand and to increase the disposal of waste through the rocks and into the sea. I think Drysdales have to be admired by the way they have enhanced access to the site and sensitively disposed of their waste, so far.)

Below the car park are a farm track, a gate and an interpretation board, which boldly states that this is 'arguably the most important geological site in the world'. The route (0.9Km) goes past the ruins of St Helen's Chapel and along the top edges of two fields to another interpretation board. You will want to look closely at the stones in the dykes here.

James Hutton set Sir James Hall the task of doing just this. The fact that there is the occasional piece of greywacke amongst the Old Red Sandstone led Hutton to decide that here was the area to look for what was to become his famous unconformity.

This second board shows how Hutton's Unconformity was formed and explains its significance. If we advance 50 metres to the cliff edge, we get a superb view of the rocks beneath. In the bay to the right, the planed-off vertical layers of greywacke form a beautifully regular series of circular arcs. To the left are great pavements of Old Red Sandstone, while directly below is the unconformity, easily picked out with the aid of the interpretation board.

Having come so far, we will want to go down, to examine closely, to touch and to take a photograph. **Proceed with care.** The slope down is as steep as a grass slope can be and may be dangerous, but down there one can roam freely along the shore. Only a fishing boat and the seabirds are likely to break the solitude.

Playfair said 'How much further reason may sometimes go than imagination can venture to follow', and we can test for ourselves his hypothesis in the very spot where Hutton, the Great Scot, expounded his great discovery.

Chapter Two

A Puzzle Solved
Ben Peach and Inchnadamph

Charles Peach was a Cornishman who served in the Revenue Coastguard, at the same time pushing himself forward in scientific circles. In 1841, he gave a paper to the British Association on *The Organic Fossils of Cornwall.* Every year thereafter, he submitted a paper and attended its meetings. Enthusiastic and outgoing, he was respected by the great men of his day. In 1853, he was promoted to Wick and began a close association with Robert Dick, the Thurso baker.

Samuel Smiles, the optimistic author of such books as *Self-help, Thrift* and *Character,* saw Dick as the perfect example of the poor man hauling himself up by his own bootstraps in the selfless pursuit of knowledge. While desperately trying to make a living, he made incredible journeys on foot, making a steady stream of discoveries. He had a distracting stream of visitors, including—at the second time of asking—Sir Roderick Murchison, Director-General of the Geological Survey of Great Britain and Director of the Royal School of Mines (now Imperial College).

Murchison complained of the lack of a decent map of Caithness, so Dick spread some flour on the baking table and proceeded to shape it into a geological model of the county, complete with hills and mountains, folds and fractures, watersheds and drainage—much of it new knowledge to the visitor who was delighted and astonished.

Ben Peach (1842-1926), son of Charles, attended Wick Academy and probably was one of the circle of boys that gathered around Dick and were inspired by him. Murchison had Peach sent to the Royal School of Mines, and he was the fourth member of staff to be appointed to the Geological Survey of Scotland, in 1862.

Enthusiastic and outgoing like his father and with John Horne, his major achievement was unravelling the mysteries of the complex geology of the North-

West Highlands, a task which took the years from 1883 till 1897, and which has stood unchallenged since.

Inchnadamph, his 'headquarters', is still a place of pilgrimage for geologists, professional and amateur, from all over the world. A truly Great Scot.

All travel stories should begin with a map. The British Geological Survey's Special Sheet of Assynt at a scale of 1:50 000 is a map of staggering complexity and many colours (see PLATE 2b). With the usual devilish ingenuity of the Ordnance and Geological Surveys, the area we are interested in, Assynt, would require four of the 'normal' OS maps at the 1:50 000 scale.

So we have the very Special Sheet of Assynt. The map area is slightly bigger than one of the regular sheets, but what catches the eye is the vast amount of additional material around the map proper. There are photographs with captions, some of them with labels, faults and thrusts superimposed in white. There are eight sections showing 'the general relationships of bedrock along the lines drawn on the map'.

There is 'a shaded terrain model with main thrusts, faults, shear zones and intrusions shown'. There is a long list of contributors to the map information, and a little map showing which areas have been updated by which contributors, and when. Absolutely critical for a geological map are the keys that identify and describe the various rocks in the area and their relationship with each other—oldest at the bottom, youngest at the top—usually, but not always in Assynt! Without going into detail, it is obvious that there is great diversity and complexity in this area.

There is a label which says, 'This map is not suitable for use in navigation'. Most things we associate with Ordnance Survey maps have been left out—houses, churches with spires, woodland, etc.—although roads can be picked out, just! Presumably, even geologists must have to find their way to the critical exposures!

An overall glance at the map shows a large area (in cream) round the south and east sides of the sheet, ending abruptly on the west. From the map it looks pretty uniform. In the south-west corner and with four 'satellites' to the north is (using slightly archaic but understandable terminology) Torridonian sandstone. The north and west (in Madder Pink) is what used to be called Lewisian gneiss, looking deceptively uniform from a distance, but traversed by a multitude of faults. This leaves, in the middle, a tangle of grey and turquoise, which is a giant puzzle, commonly known as the 'Assynt window'.

With the aid of a magnifying glass, one can just pick out the name 'Inchnadamph'. There is no town, no church, with or without a spire, nothing but a hotel, a few houses, not even a clachan, and a (closed) post office. Twenty-nine families were cleared off the land in 1819. The old church, till 1898 the parish church of Assynt, is now a café.

The old school is in private hands. The only 'hallmarks of developed urbanism' are a telephone kiosk and a post-box on a pole. Yet, the name Inchnadamph has gone around the world to be known wherever there are geologists, and the hotel flourishes from a stream of student visitors from many nations. Why?

Basically, the geology of north-west Scotland was not only a mystery but the cause of bitter controversy. Ben Peach (1842-1926) and John Horne (1848-1928), based on Inchnadamph, spent fourteen years unravelling the mysteries—'the most spectacular discovery of all time in British geology'. In the following years, their work has been supplemented and refined, but never supplanted. Geologists from every nation know of them and of Inchnadamph, and want to come and see for themselves.

Scots were prominent in the development of geological thought. James Hutton began the revolution with his conviction and explanation of the great age of the earth. Hutton found: 'no vestige of a beginning, no prospect of an end'. Charles Lyell's *Principles of Geology* was the best book on the subject for most of the 19th century. He was the first to subdivide geological time into the periods familiar to us today, and to expound the principle that 'the present is the key to the past'.

Autodidacts like Robert Dick, the Thurso baker and Hugh Miller, the Cromarty stonemason, established the fossil record and interpreted the new discoveries for the general public. Thomas Jamieson established the main phases of the Ice Age, while the Geikie brothers, Sir Archibald and James, refined and developed his findings. James Geikie's *The Great Ice Age and its Relation to the Antiquity of Man* of 1874 became the standard work on the subject for many years.

Towering over the geological landscape was Sir Roderick Impey Murchison Bt (1792-1871) KCB, DCL, FRS. FRSE, FLS, PRGS, PBA, MRIA, Director-General of the Geological Survey of Great Britain from 1855 to 1871. His reputation was founded on *The Silurian System* of 1839, the Devonian System and work in the Ural Mountains of Russia. He discovered gold in Australia from samples sent to him in London for analysis before it was known in Australia!

How can we measure fame? At least fifteen locations on Earth are named after him. There are Mount Murchisons in British Columbia and Antarctica. Also in British Columbia is Murchison Island. The Murchison Falls are in Uganda. In Western Australia, there is a Murchison River, with tributaries the Roderick River and the Impey River. There is even a Murchison crater on the Moon! There is a monument to him in the Russian city of Perm (Murchison 'created' the Permian period).

In the last decade of his life, Murchison became interested in the Northern Highlands (he was born in Easter Ross), and so entered our Inchnadamph story.

In 1819, John Macculloch published a geological account of Scotland, mainly based on coastal observation. His maps and sections were:

…both a sketch and a hopeful attempt to explain something extremely difficult to unravel. They create a simple interpretation out of impossible complexity and indeed were an excellent effort, being unchallenged by Murchison and others until about 1855. Professor James Nicol of Aberdeen (1810-1879) began the revisionism. In 1855, he accompanied Murchison in a belated visit to the North-West Highlands. He had worked with Murchison for several years on the Silurian system in the Southern Uplands, and had written a *Guide to the Geology of Scotland* without visiting the north-west.

But now he found major discrepancies between the field evidence, Murchison's field notes of 1837 and his obsession with the simple Silurian solution. Nicol came back the next and subsequent years, surveying systematically and gradually evolving an extremely complex explanation for the landscape.

It was a classic confrontation between the establishment and reformers, between the authority of Murchison, then Sir Archibald Geikie and the Geological Survey on the one hand, and the professors, independent academics and amateurs on the other. There was political manoeuvring, there were social slights and professional errors; Murchison's dominance and obsessive character being taken over by his protégé Geikie.

The reputation of the Geological Survey was tarnished. Their competence, efficiency, and certainly their authority, were seriously questioned. Taxpayers became involved and Geikie was forced into retirement in 1901.

Fortunately, Geikie's mind was not completely closed and in 1883, he set in motion a massive project of interpretation in the Highlands, headed up by Ben Peach and John Horne. Their fieldwork was completed in 1897 and their 'beautiful memoir' of 668 pages—*The Geological Structure of the North-West Highlands of Scotland*—was published in 1907.

Peach and Horne were a good team. It is always 'Peach and Horne', never 'Horne and Peach'. Peach was a brilliant illustrator and supplied the geological insights and intuition. Horne was born in Stirling and was in many ways, the stereotypical Lowland Scot. He was painstaking and methodical, and it was he who was mainly responsible for writing up their joint findings.

Photographs show that Peach was large and heavy, with a mop of fair hair, while Horne was tall and thin, carefully dressed with a favourite bowler hat he wore in the field.

Every spring, for fourteen years, the resolute pair took up residence at the Inchnadamph Hotel, sallying forth in all weathers in the toughest of environments to note and measure and take samples until the onset of winter. Ponies and gillies and a good lunch hamper would have eased the task and, no doubt after a good dinner, the evenings would have been spent, over a dram or two, tidying up the notes made during the day.

Fig 7:
The British Association Assynt Excursion of 1912 at the Inchnadamph Hotel
(British Geological Society)
Ben Peach presides genially, centre stage.

All over Scotland there are public monuments to all sorts of obscure figures, most of doubtful significance today. But the modest monument at Inchnadamph—an international tribute—fittingly testifies to the imagination and industry of two great pioneers, whose work has not been superseded in a century which saw the discovery of new planets and men walking on the Moon.

In September 1912, the British Association for the Advancement of Science met in Dundee. As a follow-on, 31 notable British and European geologists (and one American!) took part in an Assynt Excursion, led by Peach and Horne. What better tribute could have been paid to these great pioneers!

The Trail

From Inverness, there are two routes to Ledmore and Inchnadamph, almost identical in mileage. The eastern route, over two firths and the Kyle of Sutherland to Bonar Bridge and, as the A837, up the Oykell valley, is a very fine sequence of Easter Ross farmland, moor, forest and mountain. But the western route, the A835, to Garve, Ullapool and the rugged country beyond, is better for our purposes.

The mountains are higher and more dramatic, and the last twenty miles are in Peach and Horne's territory and run close to the Moine Thrust and all that that implies.

1. **The Dirrie More** is the watershed between the streams flowing to the North Sea and those falling towards the Minch and the Atlantic. Just beyond the highest point, pull into a loop of the old road on the left and look ahead (north-west). Around us are the big hills of the Moine Schists, old and rough enough, with rocky slopes but not precipitous. Ahead we get our first glimpse of the ancient Torridonian sandstone in the multiple peaks of An Teallach. Just below, note the small stream, the Abhainn Droma.

Drive down to the junction at Braemore, and turn left along the A832 to the National Trust for Scotland car park, for the Corrieshalloch Gorge and the Falls of Measach.

2. **Follow the good winding path** down to the fine modern suspension bridge, cross over and walk downstream to the viewing platform, cantilevered over the edge of the gorge.

When the author first came here, in 1947, he skipped over the old bridge and peered over the edge without a qualm. When reconnoitring for this trail, he found the vibration of the bridge, however well engineered, quite disturbing and the viewpoint even more so. The walls of the gorge are vertical, damp and deep, with ferns—no doubt rare—hanging on the sides.

Far below is the puny river and upstream, a fine waterfall. Hanging over the rail to get a good shot, there was felt a compulsion—fortunately resisted—to drop the camera into the abyss below.

How could the modest little Abhainn Droma have cut this huge slot through the mountains? The answer, of course, is that it didn't. For an explanation, we have to go back to the Younger Dryas Stadial, which we used to call the Loch Lomond Readvance—which describes it better. This was the last event in the most recent glaciation and it concluded in the most spectacular fashion.

We worry today about changes of temperature of 0.5 degree C in hundred years. Around 9500 BC, world temperatures rose a massive 7 degrees C in fifty years. As Malcolm Rider says:

The world went from ice-house to greenhouse in a generation! There would have been unimaginable flooding and chaos all across northern Scotland.

As we go back to Braemore and north towards Ullapool, we pass the massive delta of these floodwaters at the head of the glaciated valley of Loch Broom, and note that Ullapool itself is built on a huge delta of the Ullapool River coming in from the east.

The road north twists and turns. To the west, there is a sea of Lewisian gneiss, out of which rise some of the finest mountains in Britain—Cul Mor, Cul Beag, Stac Polly, Suilven, Quinag. A sign at the roadside tells us we are now entering the North West Highlands Geopark.

3. **At Knockan Crag (Chreag A'Chnocain),** we find a fine car park with good toilets, introductory information boards and an impressive 'sculpture' with the dates and samples of the rocks around us. Rider thinks that the site:

...requires a more adult display than the dumbed-down, child-appealing version chosen by SNH (Scottish Natural Heritage).

'You pays your money and you takes your choice'—but access is free!

The visitor must make up his or her own mind. My reaction is to say that the evidence and issues are so vast and complex, and the relationship of any one person to this landscape makes him or her so puny, that any approach that increases understanding must be worthwhile.

Along the road, at the Inchnadamph Hotel, an interpretation board jocularly describes how Charles Lapworth (1842-1920) suffered nightmares when staying at the hotel, imagining that the Moine Thrust was about to come crashing down and destroy everything. Lapworth was no fool but a distinguished English geologist who identified the Ordovician period and preceded Peach and Horne in investigating the north-west.

Lake Lapworth was a huge glacial lake in the Welsh borderlands and was named after Lapworth, who first suggested its existence in 1898. Lapworth's scientific career ended in nervous breakdown. Poor Lapworth's mind had grown giddy by looking so far into the abyss of time. Hardly a suitable subject for humour!

A track leads up to the Rock Room, a visitor point which blends into the hillside. Greeting us as we enter are Peach and Horne (and as we leave, we pass a contemporary geologist, with the tools of her trade). There are displays and puzzles, keyed into the surrounding landscape. A panoramic panel identifies the hills around and the touch of a button pronounces their names in Gaelic.

Three trails go on and up from here to a line of cliffs running parallel to the road. Pauses for breath are given by rock art and poetry, timescales and information boards till you get a 'chance to bridge 500 million years with your bare hands!' Before you is the white Cambrian limestone, and on top of it are the dark crystalline Moine Schists. And you can bridge the thrust plane. As Rider says:

The thrust plane is perfectly visible for some 300ft, knife sharp and simple. Incredibly, on top of this simple surface, all the rocks of the Highland mass have moved at least 50 miles. Looking at the surface, even now, it is impossible to imagine the huge mass of the Highlands sliding slowly westwards over it, rock grinding on rock, crystal shattering crystal but the geology tells us it is so.

There was a time when I could face the steepest crags with equanimity and go up hills 'like a train'. But no more, and here, on Knockan Crag, I was extremely uncomfortable. The hillside and track were steep, and above me, the black rocks of the Moine Thrust were overhanging and threatening. I had been battered by untold millions of years, and just could not get hold of the thought that all that country to the east had been creeping and sliding westwards, almost since life on this planet had begun.

I could fully understand how poor Lapworth had become deranged by the vastness of creation and man's minuscule part in it.

Back to the car and on through Elphin, where the grass on the other side really is greener, and for a good geological reason, too.

4. **OS Grid NC249142.** A private road leads off to the right, signposted 'Ledmore Marble Ltd'. Marble, strictly speaking, is metamorphosed limestone. Much of the rock in the Assynt window is mylonite, crushed rocks (including the Durness limestone), which have been forced into ribbon-like patterns.

This is an opportunity to tell the only geological joke the author knows.
Question—How fast did the Moine Thrust move?
Answer—Mylonite. (A mile a night—no wonder Lapworth was worried).

5. **Bone Caves.** From the roadside car park, follow the Allt nan Uamh (Burn of the Caves) upstream, past the former summer shielings, noting how streams appear and disappear in this limestone territory. High up on the south side of the valley is a series of caves which were first investigated by Peach and Horne in 1917 (or 1889, according to another authority).

They found two human skeletons from Neolithic times, about 6000 BC. Around their hearths, they found the bones of northern lynx, bear, reindeer and Arctic fox, as well as those of fish and animals still to be found in Scotland.

The temptation to explore the caves must be resisted. This is specialist territory and this is the biggest cave system in Scotland. In the nearby Uamh An Claonaite, divers of the Grampian Speleological Society have explored 2.868 kilometres of passages, passing deep pools, a waterslide and six sumps to reach The Great Northern Time Machine, a huge chamber large enough to contain Edinburgh's Usher Hall.

6. **Inchnadamph Hotel** has been modernised and extended since the days of Peach and Horne. Richard McKendrick, the owner, is conscious of the hotel's heritage and unique character. Practically every student of Geology in Britain spends a week here (or at the neighbouring hostel), learning their trade in the footsteps of Peach and Horne.

As well as a Mecca for geologists, Assynt is great fishing country and has some of the best mountains in the country. No doubt cavers come to the hotel to dry out and, of course, there is a constant stream of more passive tourists.

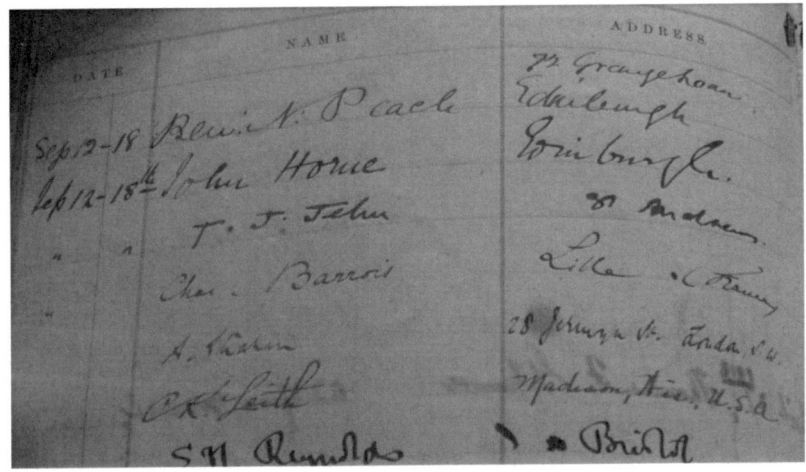

Fig 8:
Guest Book of Inchnadamph Hotel, September 1912
(Courtesy of Richard McKendrick)
Peach and Horne at the top.
On line 4, note Charles Barrois from Lille, France
and on line 6, CK Leith from Madison, Wisconsin, USA.

Further down the page are another from France (Sorbonne), two from Switzerland and one from 'St Petersburgh', plus various from Great Britain and Ireland.

The hotel displays great specimens of giant trout caught in nearby lochs. There are geological samples, maps and old photographs. For aficionados, Mr McKendrick will produce the guest book signed by Peach and Horne. The hotel must be a major contributor to the local economy, and in November 2014, Rohan Arthur McKendrick was the first child to be born in the area for thirty years.

7. **Gleann Dubh and the Allt Traligill.** The best walk from the Inchnadamph Hotel is to cross the river and follow the track that leads to Ben More Assynt and Conival. In May, you will be serenaded by 'the ceaseless rural cuckoo' as a major tributary (Allt Poll an Droighinn) bursts out of the hillside. Onwards and upwards you go, crossing limestone pavements, till you come down again to the main river.

Following it upstream, it disappears and one trudges upward in a completely dry valley, geologically confused, till one comes across the stream on the surface again.

Up here, on the left, are great banks of my favourite wild flower, *Dryas octopetala* (Mountain Avens), 'one of the most striking of alpine plants'. It has little, almost evergreen, leaves, like an oak leaf and a mass of white flowers. Although not rare, it is certainly not common, as it is dependent on a base-rich soil—and that is a rarity in the Highlands. It is a lovely little plant and, like the Edelweiss in the Alps, its attraction is enhanced by its rarity and inaccessibility.

On the south side of the valley is another series of three caves. These are more approachable than the Bone Caves and can be entered and explored with a torch, given that sensible safety precautions are followed.

8. **The Peach and Horne Monument** is a suitable conclusion to the trail. After covering some of the territory, they explored and having learnt to understand some of the processes that brought about this landscape, we can begin to understand their achievement. Their monument (PLATE 3a) is on a small hillock a hundred yards west of the A837 with a splendid view across the valley to their old watering-hole, the Inchnadamph Hotel, and the big hills of Ben More Assynt and Conival.

The plaque reads as follows:

TO
BEN N PEACH
AND
JOHN HORNE
WHO PLAYED THE FOREMOST PART IN UNRAVELLING THE
GEOLOGICAL STRUCTURE
OF THE
NORTH-WEST HIGHLANDS
1885-1897
AN INTERNATIONAL TRIBUTE
ERECTED 1930

The author began by claiming that Inchnadamph was a weel-kent place internationally for geologists. When the photograph was taken, the monument was being visited by twelve amateur and professional geologists from Jackson, Wyoming, on a two-week 'pilgrimage' to Scotland. In the car park for the Bone Caves was a Dutch fire tender and a German-registered car.

In the Traligill valley, I met two lads from Liverpool on the way to Ben More Assynt and Conival, a Dutch couple who had 'done' the Bone Caves and were now bound for the Gleann Dubh caves, and a London lad walking from Cape Wrath to Fort William. Back in the car park, a trio from Chamonix were setting off for the Traligill trail. I was the only Scot around.

Clearly, these were not all attracted by the fame of Inchnadamph, but they were all there, consciously or unconsciously, to enjoy the wildness; the key to which had been unlocked by the Great Scots Ben Peach and James Horne.

Chapter Three

A Question of Identity
Arkle and Arkle

Dozens of people, when asked about 'Arkle', stared at me as if I had just arrived from Mars, to reply, patronisingly, 'He was a racehorse and a jolly good one at that'. Which was true, but it is rather like saying that WG Grace was a good cricketer. Just as the sign outside a cricket ground would say:

CRICKET MATCH

ADMISSION THREEPENCE

IF W G GRACE PLAYS ADMISSION SIXPENCE

When Arkle raced, he was in a class of his own. Arkle did not run on the flat and did not appear at fashionable Ascot, Epsom or 'Glorious Goodwood'. He was not inbred, overbred, nervous; he did not retire to stud at 4 years old. He was able not only to run hard and fast, but to clear an assortment of fences, hurdles and ditches *en route*—usually on heavy going in winter.

Although, he was a gelding, he was a thoroughbred, born in 1957 and trained in Ireland. He was ridden throughout his steeplechasing career by an Irish jockey, Pat Taaffe.

The Timeform rating is the official 'Roll of Honour' of racing. At 212, his rating is the highest ever awarded to a steeplechaser.

Most of his races were Handicaps—races in which the handicapper tries to have all the horses crossing the finishing line together by manipulating the weight each is carrying. So the more successful Arkle became, the more weight he had to carry. Thus, when he won the Irish Grand National in 1964, it was only by one length, but he was carrying two and a half stones (16 Kg) more than the rest. Yet, despite the handicapper, out of 35 races Arkle contrived to win 27, was second only twice and was third three times.

The first time he won the Cheltenham Gold Cup, in 1964, was the last time he did not start a race as favourite, and such was the superiority of Arkle (and Mill House) that only two other horses were entered! For the Cheltenham Gold Cup in 1966 (won by 30 lengths), he started at 1/10, the shortest priced favourite in history. (Odds of one to ten mean that a stake of £10 earns you £1, but only if the horse wins.)

In Ireland, for the Irish Grand National, two weight systems were introduced—one to be used if Arkle was running and another when he wasn't. Like that other sporting genius, WG Grace, Arkle had his lovable eccentricities, one of which was to cross his forelegs when jumping a fence. This may, or may not, have contributed to his downfall at Kempton in the King George VI Chase when he hit a rail with his hoof and broke a bone.

He never ran again in competition. He was retired and ridden as a hack by his owner. At 13, he became ill and was put down.

Arkle, especially in Ireland, became a legend. His success was reputed to come from two Guinness a day. Dominic Behan wrote a song about him. 'Arkle for President' appeared on a Dublin wall. He was known as 'Himself' and fan mail arrived, addressed to 'Himself, Ireland'. (We do not know whether he replied to his fans!)

In 1981, he became the subject of a postage stamp. (In 1966, the notion had been kicked into the long grass by the Irish Parliament). Arkle's skeleton is on display in the museum of the Irish National Stud in County Kildare.

Of all those I had questioned, only one had anything original to say about 'Arkle'. She said: 'Beautiful mountain and famous horse'. Arkle (2582ft/787m) for her is a mountain in the west of Sutherland. Not particularly high—it is not a Munro—it is 181st out of the 224 Corbetts, Corbetts are Scottish hills between 2500 and 3000 feet with at least 500 feet of re-ascent on all sides. Thus Corbetts are all separate peaks and have excellent views.

Arkle is a massive mountain of Cambrian quartzite; very old, very tough and very hard on the climber's knees and feet. During the last phase of glaciation, the Loch Lomond Readvance, it was a nunatak—an Eskimo word for a peak which sticks up above the ice cover. The consequence is that the lower slopes have been eroded, rounded and smoothed by the ice, while severe frost action has shattered the upper slopes into angular quartzite blocks. (PLATE 3b)

By contrast with Arkle, the horse, Arkle, the mountain, gets a bad press from some who should have known better. The Rev AE Robertson, the first to climb all the Munros, wrote in 1907, Arkle:

…may be somewhat profanely likened to a vast shale heap, and the individual who essays to scale "the ghastly cheek of Arkle" will have an experience in rough walking he will not easily forget.

As Hamish Brown, who climbed all the Corbetts and wrote a book about them, said: 'You have been warned. If it is as bad as that it must be good'.

WA Poucher (1891-1988) was one of the best of mountain photographers. Not a macho-man but a research chemist for Yardley, described by his fellow-climbers as 'a perfume salesman who wears his wares', once revealed the story behind his iconic photograph of Liathach in the snow, from Loch Clair. He stayed at the Loch Torridon Hotel with strict instructions to the chambermaid that, if the top of Liathach was clear, he was to be wakened at 4 a.m. with a cup of tea.

It took a month, but he got his photo! His colour photo of Arkle, spread across two pages, is magnificent. The caption, however, reads: 'The latter mountain (Arkle) consisting of quartzite, is known to mountaineers as a "Slag Heap"—not worthy of exploration'.

Arthur Wainwright (1907-1991) is a name to conjure with, especially in the Lake District. A loner and a curmudgeon, he produced a stream of mountain guidebooks, hand lettered and with meticulous pen-and-ink sketches. In England, he is almost worshipped but he left Scotland till too late. In the 1970s, he produced six volumes of *Scottish Mountain Drawings.*

The sketches are as good as ever, but his comments are increasingly peevish, and it is clear he did not venture far from the main roads, and these are rare in the Highlands. I think that, by this time, he was oppressed by the size and bleakness of the Scottish wilderness. He repeats Poucher's criticism.

Incredible though it may seem, Arkle, the mountain, also appeared on a stamp. The 25th anniversary of the Investiture of the Prince of Wales was marked with an issue of commemorative stamps. The 25p stamp was of his painting of 'Ben Arkle, Sutherland, Scotland'. Pity that someone got the name wrong!

When we come to the Trail, I shall demonstrate, not only that these experts were wrong, but why they went wrong. But before then, it is necessary to answer the question—'Why should an Irish racehorse and a Scottish mountain have the same name?'

Anne Sullivan (Nancy) grew up in County Cork, becoming an excellent rider. In the World War 2, she served as a driver in the First Aid Nursing Yeomanry. In 1946, she met Hugh Grosvenor, 2nd Duke of Westminster and became his fourth wife the following year. The Duke was enormously rich, owning half of Belgravia (Grosvenor Square, etc.), Eaton Hall and much of Cheshire and a vast estate in Sutherland.

He died in 1953, and the Duchess and her stepdaughter (five years older than she) became eighth among the wealthiest landowners in Scotland.

The Duchess was passionately fond of horse racing and Arkle was bought for 1150 guineas in August 1960 in Dublin. As the owner of a promising young jumper, what could be more natural than to name him after the fine mountain on her estate? Also, on her estate was another fine mountain — Foinaven (2999ft/914m)—after which the Duchess named another horse Foinavon. More of this later.

The Trail

Climbing Arkle is not like a ramble in the Cotswolds. It is a serious business. The Westminster estate office is at Achfary on the A838, and permission is usually given to take a car up the private road to Lone (GR309422), saving 2-3Km on the day. Looking north-east from Lone, a good stalker's path heads for the valley of the Allt Horn, which separates Arkle on the left from Meall Horn on the right.

Arkle is quartzite and rugged while Meall Horn is more subdued. The river follows the edge of the Moine Thrust, where everything from the east has been thrust over the Cambrian and Pre-Cambrian rocks.

The 'tourist route' to Arkle follows the stalker's path for just over a mile (1.5Km), then turns north up heather and stony slopes to Meall Aonghais. Bare stony slopes lead to the summit ridge, which leads to the actual summit after a mile. The guidebook time for the ascent from Lone is two hours and forty minutes.

For the connoisseur, there is a much better route. From Lone, head due north, angling upwards along the lower edges of Arkle's scree slopes and turning uphill to follow a burn up to and beyond its source (see PLATE 3b). The going is tough over the frost-shattered quartzite, but just before one arrives at the lowest point of the ridge, is a large spread of Moss Campion (*Silene acaulis*), and then one is in for a shock!

Arkle could be compared to a vast plum pudding. We have been climbing up the convex side of the pudding and we now find that the distant half of the pudding has been scooped away by a giant bite. We are standing on a narrow ridge. Before us is a great void and beyond that, the magnificence of Foinaven.

Arkle is a big mountain, but Foinaven is an even bigger mountain, in every way. It is higher; so high that it is almost a Munro, and every now and then, it is re-measured to see if it can be made to be the magic 3000ft or 914.4 metres. (Isostatic uplift, the recovery of northern Scotland from the weight of the ice, is sure to elevate Foinaven—but when? And will the rise in sea level as a result of global warming negate the isostatic uplift?)

Foinaven has a huge central spine with ridges coming off it and these are of frost-shattered blocks of Cambrian quartzite, defended by great masses of scree. The view from Arkle is raw and almost terrifying. A pavement of ice-moulded Lewisian gneiss has a multitude of little lochans glinting in the sun, and out of it arises this great, tough monolith. Compare this with the rich green of The Curragh or Cheltenham—a highly-strung racehorse could not last five minutes here!

The last mile to the summit of Arkle is:

…a magnificent curving ridge, which is narrow and rough going for one short stretch along a natural pavement of quartzite.

Not a place for the inexperienced in a high wind or in snow and ice.

The return journey is by the 'tourist route'—no heroics.

Footnote

Foinavon deserves a mention. Clearly not a patch on Arkle, he still has his place in racing history. The Grand National has always been notorious for the length of the race, the number and difficulty of the jumps and by the large fields entered for the race. (The Duchess never entered Arkle for the Grand National, in case he got injured or killed.)

The National has always been unpredictable, but the 1967 race was completely topsy-turvy and probably the most dramatic ever. There were 44 starters and one, Popham Downs, unseated its rider at the first fence but, as such loose horses often do, continued to run and jump with the herd.

At the 23rd fence (the smallest fence on the course), there were still 28 horses with jockeys competing, when Popham Downs 'refused', cannoned into another horse and at least six or seven horses fell, refused, or were brought down. Horses ran up and down the fence, blocking others and some even began running back the way they had come.

Foinavon was not a great horse. His owner had not even bothered to come to the course. The odds on him were 100/1—in other words, if you put a bet on him of £1 each way and, by some miracle, he won, you would be paid £127. And there was a miracle!

Foinavon was so far back that he missed the melée. His jockey, John Buckingham, quickly sized up the situation, coolly steered his horse round the chaos and jumped on the outside. At the Canal Turn, Buckingham (the fourth choice for the ride) looked back to find he held a 30-length lead over 17 remounted horses with only six fences to go. He managed to hang on to win by 20 lengths.

The jockey's comment on his mount was:
He was a lovely old fella. Nice and quiet, very reliable and honest. He was a nine-year-old, a good age for a Grand National horse.

Buckingham won two more races on Foinavon, but retired (through injury) after riding 98 winners.

One is reminded of Aesop's Fable of *The Tortoise and The Hare.* Foinavon is not forgotten—the 23rd fence was renamed Foinavon in 1984. The supreme irony was that the Duchess of Westminster had obviously decided that this horse was no good and had sold it to Cyril Watkins.

It may be asked what my qualifications are for writing about Arkle and the world of National Hunt racing, since my only real success was in 1953, when I backed Knock Hard to win the Cheltenham Gold Cup—which he did? However, through life, I have been blessed with good luck and latterly, this must have been the result of rubbing Arkle's horseshoe in the Arkle Bar of the Londonderry Arms Hotel, Carnlough, County Antrim. (The Duke of Westminster was a special friend of Winston Churchill, who owned the hotel.)

And I have climbed Arkle, the mountain, carefully traversing the 'bad step' on the final ridge.

An Afterthought

Some might be concerned that Arkle has been categorised as a Great Scot. After all, he was born in Ireland, trained in Ireland and worshipped in Ireland. His owner was Irish. She married an Englishman. Only when her husband died, did she become the owner of a Scottish estate. So what made Arkle Scottish?

The answer lies in his name. Hyperion might suit a Derby winner, but not a rough and tumble jumper. Marmaduke Jinks is just so trivial. But Arkle is such a tough and challenging Norse name for a tough and challenging mountain that it suited the toughest and best of horses. The name itself is so apposite that it must have helped to make Arkle a Great Scot.

Chapter Four

Known World-wide
Sir Humphrey Davy and Strontian

Sir Humphrey Davy (1778-1829) was probably the leading scientist of his time. A native of Penzance, he trained as a doctor and chemist before busying himself in several branches of science. He determined to study and graduate at Edinburgh, but never quite got round to it, being too busy doing great things in Bristol.

It was 1799 before he first got round to visiting London. Contact with Scotland was minimal. He painted Loch Lomond twice around 1796, and was elected President of the Royal Society on St Andrews Day, 1820.

He made many practical discoveries and inventions. We remember best the Davy Safety Lamp, which prevented the deaths of thousands of miners, and which he refused to patent. In the midst of much else, he was the first to isolate new elements—magnesium, boron, barium, iodine, sodium and potassium—by electrolysis. In a lecture to the Royal Society on 30 June 1808, he announced his latest discovery, naming it Strontium.

Davy could without question be called a Great Cornishman. How could be called a Great Scot? When he isolated the new elements, he gave them names in a certain style. Barium was New Latin from a Greek root—a creation. Boron came from Old French, which came from Medieval Latin, which came from Arabic, which came from Persian—another creation. Iodine was French, from Greek. Magnesium was New Latin from Medieval Latin, from Greek. Potassium was from New Latin potassa, for potash, while sodium was New Latin from Medieval Latin—both creations.

Strontium was his only discovery to be named after a place and not from the history of science. My suggestion is that this recognised a special affinity that Davy felt for his Scottish discovery, and this qualifies him to be a Scot by association or, as in cricket, special registration. He did not have a Scottish granny, but he certainly had a Scottish relationship.

Some twenty-nine minerals were first described as being from Scotland. Most were pretty rare, like lanarkite, brewsterite and leadhillite. One with an interesting pedigree was strontianite. In 1790, Adair Crawford, a physician working with barium, noted that, associated with veins of gneiss in certain lead mines in Argyll, 'the scotch mineral is a new species of earth which has not hitherto been sufficiently examined'. Sulzer and Blumenbach named the mineral strontianite and confirmed that it was, indeed, new to science.

Strontium is 38 in the Periodic Table. It is one of the group of Alkaline Earth Metals which are Beryllium (4), Magnesium (12), Calcium (20), Strontium (38), Barium (56), and Radium (88). They have a shared chemistry and a clear trend in properties. Strontianite is quite rare and few deposits have been found that are suitable for development.

But strontium is the 15th most abundant element on Earth, mainly in the form of celestite (strontium sulphate). Strontium is softer than calcium, reacts with water and burns in air, requiring that it be stored in oil. (One of the best fun things in school chemistry used to be to watch a lump of magnesium—another of the family—dashing around a tank of water generating fire and steam.)

In the 19th century, strontium was used in large quantities in the sugar beet industry. A principal use in the 20th century, now mainly superseded, was for cathode ray tubes in television sets. Strontium carbonate is used to give fireworks a deep red colour. Strontium-90 is a radioactive isotope created during nuclear explosions or in nuclear reactors in the process of fission of heavy nuclei.

As a Good Friend, it is used in the treatment of bone cancer. As a Bad Master, it became a major political problem during the atmospheric tests of nuclear weapons carried out in the 1950s by the US, the Soviet Union, and Britain. So notorious did it become that Novaya Zembla (the large island north of Siberia used for testing) appeared in the O Grade Geography paper as a place to be identified! Sr-90 was an important component of the fallout that was deposited all over the world, but in 1963, the US, the Soviet Union, and Great Britain signed a treaty banning atmospheric testing.

However, with the disintegration of the Soviet Union, the system for keeping track of Sr-90 power sources fell into some disarray. The accident at the Chernobyl nuclear power plant introduced a large amount of Sr-90 into the environment. A large part of this Sr-90 was deposited in the Soviet Republics. The rest was dispersed as fallout over Northern Europe and worldwide.

So, despite the crimson brilliance of stable strontium, its radioactive variety has given element 38 an air of risk and notoriety.

When James VI, King of Scots, attained adulthood, he set about taking control of the Highlands and Islands. On Elizabeth of England's death, he cleared up the borders, shipping off the malcontents in what is generally known as the Plantation of Ulster. Chiefs and lairds at home were now members of a more peaceable society and could devote themselves to developing their estates—improving their lands in whatever way seemed likely to be profitable.

Those with estates near the sea headhunted families from north Germany and Denmark to develop fisheries. Some turned to coal-mining. Others sought greater riches.

Associated with the Dalradian and Moinian, granites of the Caledonian mountain-building episode of 1,000—540 million years ago are some rare, and even precious, metals. The Romans used a lot of lead and certainly mined it in, what we now call, County Durham. They may have exploited the Leadhills-Wanlockhead area. With lead, there are often small quantities of silver. Even smaller quantities of gold can be found, enough for knowledgeable locals to find to make a wedding ring for a local bride.

Coal-mining, once the coal is found, is fairly straightforward. The workable seams are usually of uniform thickness and mostly predictable. Once extracted, coal requires little more processing. The mining of the rarer metals is not straightforward. The deposits are in veins or agglomerations which may run out at any time, and the proportion of waste to valuable deposit is much higher.

(It could be said that coal-mining was merely brute labour, while lead-mining required a higher level of intelligence. Certainly, when one looks at the catalogue of the Miners' Library in Wanlockhead, one is knocked sideways by the spread and seriousness of the miners' reading in earlier centuries). Mineral deposits in the Highlands are infrequent and limited.

As a result, the cost of mining lead is higher. Little lead or silver occurs in metallic form, so the first task after mining is to crush and smelt the ore. On the other hand, lead, silver and gold fetch much higher prices than equivalent weights of coal.

Events far from the mine can have devastating results. I have stood on the edge of the world's largest copper 'mine', near Salt Lake City, and looked down at trucks the size of ladybirds crawling along the bottom of a hole which was once a mountain. Close up, the tyres of these trucks were twenty feet high! How could an enterprise like Strontian compete with a resource like this?

In the 19th century, there was a world shortage of gold until it was discovered in California, Alaska, Australia, New Zealand, and South Africa. There were gold rushes and any little home producers were put out of business. In 1972, *The Ecologist* in *Blueprint for Survival* forecast that there were only ten years supply of lead left in the world.

Did the price of lead shoot up? Were old mines bought up and re-opened? Not at all. The main use of lead was in petrol for cars, and some clever people worked out how lead-free petrol could be as efficient as leaded, so that use of the latter just withered away, as did that particular doomsday prediction!

Production costs and market prices come from many sources, many of them out of the reach of the miners and the result is that prospecting and exploitation are a chancy business—as the history of Strontian will show.

In 1714, Sir Alexander Murray of Stanhope, a keen mineralogist, bought the estates of Sunart and Ardnamurchan because of their economic potential. (Stanhope is at the centre of the lead-mining district of County Durham, but I do not *know* that Murray came from that Stanhope). In 1722, the lead-mines at Strontian were leased by Sir Archibald Grant, General George Wade (busily engaged in road-building in the Highlands) and others.

In 1730, the estate, including the mines, was taken over by The Governor and Company for raising the Thames Water at York Buildings (aka the York Buildings Company). But what on earth was a London water company up to in the remote fastnesses of the Western Highlands?

To quote David Murray in *The York Buildings Company: A Chapter in Scotch History*.

No name is more familiar to the Scotch lawyer than that of the York Buildings Company; and many a one, puzzled by its perpetual recurrence in the pages of textbooks and reports, has asked, and often asked in vain, what this litigious company was, or what possible connection it could have with Scotland?

After the 1715 Rebellion, the estates of the Jacobite leaders were confiscated by the government and sold off. After some extremely murky business, which is completely beyond the author's understanding, the company took over several estates in Scotland, some of which were ruthlessly exploited and others mismanaged. Again, to quote Murray:

It is a peculiarity of joint-stock enterprise that the fields in which it is to gather golden harvests are, like the gardens of the Hesperides, generally far from home and their whereabouts only dimly ascertainable.

The first manager at Strontian, Francis Place, a Quaker, started well. 'The works every day grow richer since I came here', he reported. Colonel Horsey wrote to Place: 'Under your management, we shall find great riches'. In the first two or three years, £40,000 were spent.

New furnaces and smelting mills were built. Almost daily ships brought in bricks and castings, coals and timber. 'Framed houses' were brought in from London. Oatmeal and malt—for there was no satisfactory local surplus of food—were imported. A village known as New York was built and 500 workmen were said to be employed.

Yet, all was not well. The company 'never drew as much for its lead sold as would pay the wages of the workmen'. The meal—porridge was the staple diet of the miners—was 'like to run out, and we are almost reduced to short allowance'. At Leadhills, there was scurvy in winter, due to lack of green vegetables, and at Strontian:

The men begin to be apprehensive of the sickness which is customary in the winter, and it is with great difficulty, that I keep the smelters, which are in tolerable health.

The company's organisation was a colony forced upon a local population with their own problems. 'The Highlanders were a source of alarm' and at one point (via General Wade), troops were requested. Money ran short and miners' wages fell into arrears. In 1735, the unpaid miners took possession of the lead ore.

Despite all this, the company staggered along until 1815, producing £4,000 per annum, no doubt kept going by the great demand for lead bullets in the twenty years of war against France, and perhaps, the cheap labour of French prisoners of war. A big contract must have been the roofing of the new Inveraray Castle with 60 tons of Strontian lead in 1753.

In 1828, Strontian ('at one time a filthy clachan') underwent a total revolution 'under the direction of Sir James Riddell and his lady'. After the Disruption of 1843, the members of the newly formed Free Church decided they needed a church of their own in which to worship. Sir James was a staunch Episcopalian and refused to give land for a site.

However, the zealous locals obtained a ship and anchored it in a bay a mile west of Strontian village. The 'Floating Church' was used for worship from 1846 till 1873, when the laird was so impressed by the religious dedication of the congregation, that he relented and allowed a good stone church to be built on his land.

However, Sir James was not impervious to other needs of his tenants. Around 1830, he established 'The Strontian Straw Hat' factory as a means of 'improving the conditions of the peasantry on his estate'. Upwards of fifty females were employed when the scheme 'far suppressed expectations', balancing employment in the male-based economy. The enterprise probably collapsed with a change in fashion.

The gross over-population of Ireland, the dependence on the potato, the potato blight and the Great Famine are everyday knowledge. Less common is the realisation that something similar happened in the West Highlands and Islands at the same period. Robert Somers wrote a series of *Letters from the Highlands (after the Great Potato Famine of 1846)*. When he came to Loch Sunart, he found that:

The people are extremely poor, and the digging and manuring of their crofts must be a task of almost superhuman drudgery.

The lead mines of Strontian have been the means of concentrating a greater population on this spot than could otherwise have existed. But they form at the best a very precarious source of employment. At the time of my visit, forty or fifty men were employed in them: but the manager had given out that he would shortly require about 500. He complains, however, that the Highlanders are bad workers, and threatens to bring in a colony of Irish!

As late as 1886, there were still said to be differences between the crofters of Anaheilt, which consisted 'of some renovated turf huts' and the miners of Scotstown, with 'neat slated cottages of granite'. For evidence from a primary source, I turned to the Census Enumerators' Schedules, held in the Scottish Record Office.

Ardnamurchan is a huge parish divided, for census purposes, into sections. 'Sunart and Strontian' (505-03) is one of these and is, in turn, divided into Enumeration Districts. For 1871, Enumeration Districts 001-004 are held, but District 005—which comprises Strontian, Scotstown and Anaheilt—is missing from the index and from the shelves.

District 004 is immediately west of 005 and is of some help. The area 'abounds to a vast extent with high rugged hills', and was rented out as 3 sheep farms. In it were 14 houses with 42 windowed rooms, 38 males and 35 females. Anything over one person per windowed room is considered to be overcrowding, so that this little area at 1.7 was definitely overcrowded. Only one child was 'receiving instruction'. (The Education (Scotland) Act did not come into force until 1872).

There was, however, a link with the lead mines. Samuel Alexander Walton (43), born in Cumberland, England, was a mine agent. As part of management, Walton would not have thought it necessary to live cheek by jowl with the workers, nor to live next to mines and smelters. Duncan McMillan (47) was a miner and a native of Strontian.

For 1881, we find Anaheilt and Scotstown in District 003. The Enumerator worked from south to north so that the first 29 schedules are for Anaheilt and the next 52, for Scotstown. The 29 houses in Anaheilt had 58 rooms. There were 81 males and 69 females, meaning that 150 persons were seriously overcrowded at 2.6 per room.

The stated occupations of the township were blacksmith (2), joiner, shoemaker (2), tailor, salesman. There was a mail contractor and a family of three letter carriers. (The author's 'Man in Strontian', Ian Campbell informed him that this family and their descendants were known as 'Cameron Post' and that one walked twice a week to and from Kingairloch, 10Km each way over some of the toughest territory in these islands, or 25Km by road).

The Anaheilt men were also crofters. A McPhee (56) was recorded as a lead miner, but was probably trying to live off his croft. 12 of the household were Camerons. Almost all were natives of Strontian, except for one Cameron immigrant from Ardgour—the next parish to the east!

The first two entries for Scotstown were for a shop, run by 60-year-old Leitch, born in Tobermory and the Parish Manse, with Mr McLean, the minister (43), born in Ardgour, his wife, 3 children, 2 servants and a nurse.

In the rest of Scotstown, there were 52 households with 124 rooms.

There were 97 males and 107 females, with the result that 204 persons were overcrowded at 1.6 per room. Bad enough, but not so bad as in Anaheilt, where the houses were smaller and older.

The occupations were quite varied. The enumerators recorded what the subjects said they were. There were 13 lead miners recorded, 10 crofters and 9 labourers, and no unemployed or retired. It is likely that these three categories were interchangeable. Almost every household was a croft, a man who had not gone underground since 1871, might still consider himself a miner, while his neighbour found work as a labourer.

30 women were recorded as servants or housekeepers. A few of these may have been young girls on holiday or 'between jobs', but most were simply the wives or widows of householders. There was one shooting lodge up the Strontian glen, accounting for 3 gamekeepers and 5 shepherds. It was surprising to note quite a diversity of craft employment—4 laundresses, 3 dressmakers, 3 shoemakers, 3 masons, a clerk and a merchant—but it is impossible at this distance to say to what extent they were fully occupied.

There was real evidence of poverty and distress. Anne McPhee (50) was an unmarried pauper lunatic in a one-roomed 'Poorhouse'. Margaret (50) and Morag (58) were unmarried pauper sisters in a one-roomed cottage. Morag McLachlan (60) was also in a one-roomed cottage. Mary McPherson (60) shared a one-roomed house with her pauper sister (Christina, 40, unmarried) and nephew, Duncan (2), born in Glasgow.

Is there a scandal behind these facts? The sad tale of the servant, seduced by the master when his family was 'doon the watter' on holiday, and then thrown out on the street without a character?

Conditions were poor. Crime was not unknown, with some quite high-profile cases ending up at the Assizes in Oban. Animosity between the two townships did exist.

The Scotstown population was remarkably homogenous in that all, but 17 out of 124 were born in Argyll and 3 of the 17 hailed from Moidart in Invernessshire, a mere 10Km north, as the eagle flies.

Next, the author went to the census of 1891 to see whether there were any substantial changes between the two communities on 5-6 April 1891. Unfortunately, the appropriate volume of Census Enumerators' Schedules did not differentiate between Scotstown and Anaheilt; apart from nine houses in 'The Row', it was a case of 'Crofter's House' after 'Crofter's House' after 'Crofter's House'. Nevertheless, the census gives an interesting picture of the conditions up the Strontian river valley, twenty years after cessation of the mining.

There were 48 houses in Scotstown, with a total of 98 windowed rooms. The kirk manse had 11 rooms, so the rest of the township had 47 houses with 87 rooms. In them resided 79 males and 90 females, 169 in total in 87 rooms, almost two persons per room. Overcrowding was, if anything, worse than in 1891.

Over 90% of the residents were born in Argyll. 131 were speakers of Gaelic and English, and 25 spoke only Gaelic. Those who had no English were either children under 5 (who would be forced to learn English at school) or the elderly. Three of those were paupers. We can picture Donald (57) and Jessie McCall (59), a crofter and his housekeeper/sister, natives of Strontian, in their wee but-and-ben, left behind in a changing world.

In the group of 1- or 2-roomed houses, known as 'The Row', were five old ladies living alone, unmarried and paupers. Two of them spoke no English.

Ian Campbell, the 'Man in Strontian', is one of the last two Gaelic speakers in Strontian. He remembers 'The Row' as 'The Poor House', and the last occupants—Mary Gordon and her mother. The Gordons were originally from Skye and had come over as shepherds.

Mary's brothers, James and Adam, were both killed in World War I, aged, respectively, 19 and 21, one at Ypres and the other at the Somme. This loss virtually killed their father, and Mary (who never married) spent her life looking after her mother. When she died, Mary was rehoused in a small cottage nearby and the Poor House was demolished.

There was little evidence of involvement with lead mining. Two men, aged 64 and 49, described themselves as 'lead miner unemployed'. The main occupation was crofting, but as many of the holdings were half-crofts, this would have been a precarious existence. Many of them must have been lead miners who stayed on when the mines closed. The next biggest group were 'labourers'.

There were some shepherds on the cleared lands and a few gamekeepers serving the sporting estates. The interesting little collection of trades and services noted in 1881 had died out, or was so trivial as not to be recognised as worth recording. There had been a shop, but this was now closed. A pretty dismal picture.

The 500 workers were never needed as great mineral discoveries in North and South America, in South Africa, Australia and New Zealand brought down metal prices. The population of Strontian fell from 803 in 1871 to 691 ten years later.

In the 1970s, North Sea oil brought some activity back to the lead mines. Strontian Minerals Ltd began going over the old spoil heaps and mining barytes for use in drilling mud for the oil industry, with some associated lead, zinc and silver.

That phase is now over and Strontian's main source of income is now tourism, as a gateway to Ardnamurchan and the west, and with a great wealth of scenery and natural history.

The Trail

On the assumption that most travellers to Strontian will be from the South, Crianlarich is a very suitable place at which to begin to absorb the Highland landscape.

1. At **Dalrigh** ('the king's field', where Bruce defeated the Macdougalls), a track leads up the glen to Cononish, where lead and associated metals were mined for centuries. Around are varied vestiges of mining, now mainly camouflaged by forest, while the river shows tailings—traces of having been used for washing out minerals. The *Ordnance Gazetteer of Scotland* of 1881 said:

Lead mines, belonging to the Marquis of Breadalbane on the top of a hill ¾ of a mile WSW, employed over 100 men in 1839, but are now discontinued.

This was the same pattern as at Strontian, with the problem of fluctuating metal prices.

However, in 2010, Scotgold Resources was floated, and now own what is being called the Argyll gold and silver mine. Location in the Trossachs National Park was a planning issue but permission was given for 24-hour working, cutting the cost of production. The price of gold was $1,600 per ounce in 2010 and dropped to $1,100. Subsequently, there was some loss of investor enthusiasm but we were assured that the venture would be viable down to a gold price of $700.

The first sales of gold to the jewellery trade in Scotland averaged £4,558 per ounce, and in February 2018, it was decided that, instead of merely recycling existing stockpiles, an existing mine shaft would be developed.

Covid-19 shut down the mine and restricted access to suppliers, consultants and new staff but in 2021, came a turnaround in fortunes with record-breaking monthly returns. In August 2022, the operation was securely established as a high-grade, gold production company with around 80 employees. In the words of Phil Day, the chief executive with experience in Nevada, Australia, Brazil, etc.—'It is making money, there's lots of gold, we are employing very happy people'.

Another good sign was the recognition, in November 2022, of the resident geologist, Rachel Paul, as one of the 100 Global Inspirational Women in Mining. But, as a reminder of the chancy nature of gold mining, in March 2023 the headline was: 'Shares in Cononish gold mine fall sharply after challenging period.' The winter weather had been 'harsher-than-expected'.

Just before leaving Tyndrum and just over the bridge over the burn, turn left into **Clifton**—a row of miners' cottages, some renovated, some gentrified and some new build on older plots.

And it's off along the A82, over the Black Mount and Moor of Rannoch, and through Glencoe to Corran Ferry and Ardgour—a splendid run through some of the best glaciated scenery in these islands. The Moor is where the ice accumulated and pushed out in all directions. Now it is a web of seemingly formless streams and lochans, framed by a dozen major mountains. There are rocks stripped by ice, U-shaped valleys which may hold ribbon lakes or end in deep sea lochs.

Loch Linnhe is the southern end of the Great Glen Fault, which separates the north-west from the rest of Scotland. It almost beggars the imagination that all this mass of north-west Scotland has been dragged sixty miles horizontally.

Safely over the Corran Ferry, it is round the coast to Glen Tarbert, over the Allt A'Chothruim (see later) to the village of Strontian. It is a pleasant enough place, but with little evidence of its former importance. It has an hotel, a kind of green, an old bridge and a scattering of houses in a succession of styles—19th century stone villages and cottages, 1930s arts and crafts, recent bungalows and kit houses. It is only when we cross the river and follow it north, that we can follow anything we could call a trail.

2. **Anaheilt and Scotstown.** The road was built by Sir James Riddell, who made sure that the crofters at Anaheilt were relocated further up the hill, away from floods and also out of sight of the laird and his lady on their way to church. Virtually, all of the original crofts have been renovated and replaced, although behind, much higher up, stone byres remain which were used for cattle and storage.

Scotstown was where the miners lived, being allocated half-crofts to ensure a decent diet. (At Leadhills and Wanlockhead, the miners suffered from scurvy as it was too high and cold for the cultivation of vegetables.) Almost all of the 'neat slated cottages of granite' have gone. Properties have been rebuilt and gentrified, but there are fragments of masonry and the occasional ruin still to be seen.

> 2a. The enthusiast will want to branch off to the right (east) just before Scotstown, to Ariundle (Airigh = summer shielings) and the Sunart Atlantic Oakwoods, a Special Area of Conservation. A bicycle will help as the road deteriorates into a track as it rises through the forest. After 4Km, one emerges from the forest on to the open hillside and a further kilometre takes one to what the Ordnance Survey says is **Lead Mine** (rems of).
>
> These were the Bellsgrove lead mines—six or seven ruined buildings on either side of a substantial burn which would have driven some of the processing machinery. Pity the poor miners who had to trudge up from Ariundle in the foulest of weather, or over the 2Km of trackless hillside from the road above.
>
> Beyond Scotstown and near Bellsgrove Lodge, there is evidence for activity ancient and modern. There are old mine entrances and spoil heaps associated with former Middleshope Mine. Near Bellsgrove Lodge, a massive earth-moving job is going on.
>
> 3. **Further up, on the left,** is a tortured landscape of fragments of masonry, tracks in the oddest of places and villainous-looking holes, with the occasional rhododendron which has escaped from Bellsgrove Lodge. A locked gate bans access to the former Whiteside Mine, but it is easily circumvented to gain access to a sordid assemblage of rusting machinery, rotting concrete blocks and chaotic spoil heaps, the legacy of the recent barytes phase. A great excavation does not invite close inspection.

We are officially warned that this site is dangerous and the trespassing visitor must decide whether or not close inspection is worth the risk.

At the top of the hill leading to Loch Shiel (at 342 metres), take a look at the magnificent panorama in all directions. There is a tangle of rugged mountains with Ben Resipol and Ardnamurchan dominant in the west. It is a watery landscape with a multitude of freshwater lochs, feeding into long sea-lochs like Loch Sunart and the Atlantic. Extensive forests of conifers and oak fill what narrow valleys are left.

But down to the west, man's handiwork is less pleasant to look upon. The scars of lead mining can be seen to follow the veins of lead ore for about five miles along the moorland. We can't blame the Victorians for this; the worst damage has been done in the last thirty years.

On a good day, this is one of the finest places to be in the whole country, especially as the sun is setting. But on the sadly frequent days of rain and mist, looking at the rocky and steep landscape, one becomes depressed at the thought of having to make a living from such hostile territory.

There are two diversions which could be used to supplement the trail and will certainly add to an understanding of the area and its history.

4a. Just east of Strontian, the A884 crosses the Carnoch River, going along the south side of Loch Sunart, mainly as a single track with passing places, before climbing south and heading for Lochaline (opposite Mull) in a magnificently engineered succession of curves and straights. The road is a delight for the tourist and has three points which add depth to our study of the area.

After about 3Km, one has a **good view** of Strontian and its mountainous hinterland. Also, we can see the bay where the Floating Church was anchored and ministered to the spiritual needs of the Free Kirkers.

At **Lurga** (Grid Reference 733554), there are quite considerable remains, I am told, of another lead mine.

One of the two main levels is still accessible for 20 yards, but otherwise, the workings are blocked by water. Dam, washing floor, hearths and smithy are traceable.

There are stretches of pony track running down to Loch Sunart at Liddesdale (The Highlands were cleared for Cheviot sheep and it was Borderers who took them there), where the Morvern Mining Company built a handsome dwelling house for their manager, clerks and office.

Output seems to have been about a ton of lead per year, which does not seem much.

Unfortunately, Lurga is not at all easy to access from the road and even a view of it is denied by the only patch of woodland for miles!

About 3 miles short of Lochaline, turn right and follow the shore road past Loch Arienas to the car park for the historic village of **Aoineadh Mor** (pronounced Inniemore). This is Forestry Commission territory and they have done a good job in revealing the remains of a deserted Highland village—the houses, corn drying kiln, kailyard and other outbuildings. All very good, but there are dozens of deserted clachans in the Highlands. What makes Aoineadh Mor special is that we have quite a lot of detail about the settlement and its demise.

Aoineadh Mor was never a big place; in 1779, 45 Camerons lived there. In 1824:

Miss Christina Stewart of Edinburgh purchased the Glenmorvern estate from George, 6th Duke of Argyll. She ordered the eviction of the entire population, not even giving them time to stop and milk their goats. She wanted the land to graze for sheep.

The families had no official lease and so had to leave, climbing the steep hill out of the glen. Mary (Cameron) took her baby and two small children while her husband, James, carried his own mother on his back up the steep track. Before they were even halfway up the hill, their village was being destroyed behind them.

As a traditional Gaelic poem says:

Some went across the ocean.
Some went to the graveyard,
Where are the others?
No one knows.

Some of the men may have tried to get work at the lead mines, but whatever skills they may have had, would not have extended to those of the cunning miner.

The 1851, census recorded just two people at Aoineadh Mor, presumably the lowland shepherds.

A melancholy place, Aoineadh Mor, where one contemplates 'Man's inhumanity to Man'.

4b. For the motorist visiting the Highlands, there can scarcely be a better excursion from Fort William than a tour of Ardgour and Moidart, to the Corran

Ferry and over (sea) Loch Linnhe to cross the Allt A'Chothruim, to (sea) Loch Sunart and Strontian. Then over the hill to Acharacle and (freshwater) Loch Shiel, and on to (sea) Loch Moidart, Eilean Shona and (sea) Loch Ailort. On past (freshwater) Loch Eilt to Glenfinnan, Prince Charlie's monument and the head of Loch Shiel.

The final stage takes one along the shore of (sea) Locheil, through Corpach and over the Caledonian Canal to Fort William. This circuit of 75 miles (120Km) takes in magnificent mountain scenery, splendid rivers and waterfalls, a glorious mixture of land, sea, islands and views, besides the human interest of clan warfare, the beginning and end of Bonnie Prince Charlie's attempt to seize the throne and Victorian triumphs of engineering.

The motorist, if (s)he is still interested in Strontian, should stop off in Corpach and visit 'Treasures of the Earth', a commercial attraction of great interest. It claims to be 'Europe's finest private collection of Crystals, Gemstones and Fossils'. Outside, it is a huge shed. Inside, it is an Ali Baba's cavern—'an atmospheric simulation of caves, caverns and mining scenes' with giant crystals and fossils ranging from insects in amber to 'vicious prehistoric monsters'. There is real gold and silver, petrified wood, rubies, diamonds and emeralds.

There is a chance to see large specimens of minerals from the Strontian mines, which may have been looked for unsuccessfully in the old spoil heaps.

Chapter Five

An Inconspicuous Place
JK Charlesworth and Corrom (Chothruim)

John Kaye Charlesworth (1889-1972) was a Yorkshireman who graduated BSc at Leeds, lectured in Geology at Queen's University in Belfast. In Breslau (Germany), he obtained a PhD in Geography, then came back to Leeds where he was awarded a DSc. He transferred to Manchester as a senior lecturer before returning to Queen's as a full professor, as which he served from 1921 till 1954.

In 1957, he was made CBE for 'his services to Northern Ireland with particular reference to the field of geography'. His career pattern was more like that of the medieval wandering scholar than the target-driven researcher of today, and although, he was elected a Fellow of the Royal Society of Edinburgh in 1950 and awarded their Neill Prize for 1951-53, there seems little so far in his CV to justify calling him a Great Scot.

James Geikie (1839-1915) was a Great Scot whose *The Great Ice Age and its Relation to the Antiquity of Man* was 't'best book on t'soobject' of glaciation in the 19th century. Charlesworth's *The Quaternary Era, with special reference to its glaciation* was published in 1957 by Edward Arnold of London. This magisterial work of two volumes and 1700 pages was the culmination of a lifetime's research and cogitation and became the glaciation Bible for the 20th century.

When we consider the ice cover during the most recent glacial episode, about 20,000 years ago, we find that most of Ireland was covered, apart from the most southerly third. Wales was similar, with an ice-free southerly third. In England, East Yorkshire, Lincolnshire and everywhere south of the Midlands were ice-free. But everywhere in Scotland was under ice, at least 2,000 feet thick, except in the north-west where a few mountain peaks peeped above the ice.

These, like Arkle, are known as 'nunataks'—an Eskimo word. For Charlesworth, Scotland was the main focus of his book and the main source for his examples. His commitment and involvement were enough, in my book, to qualify him to be a Great Scot, by association and residence.

Ben, glen and loch are all topographical terms in Gaelic which have passed into standard English with English spelling. An armchair-shaped hollow, usually north-facing, in glaciated territory is called, in geography textbooks, a corrie (Gaelic), cwm (Welsh) or cirque (French), reflecting the environments in which such features are common. There is no English word because there was no need for one.

The first letters of the Greek alphabet are Alpha, Beta, Gamma and Delta. If one looks at a map of Egypt in a good atlas, one sees the Nile flowing from south to north as a ribbon through the desert. Near Cairo, 100 miles from the Mediterranean, the river changes character. For thousands of years, it has brought down silt, so that the coastline bulges out to the north.

Also the Nile has broken up into many distributaries, so that the river does not end with a single mouth but in a fan-shaped—delta. The Greeks called this area a delta and the symbol for the letter Delta became a triangle.

Although, many rivers run straight into the sea or into a lake, many rivers carry silt and stones downstream to form a delta, and deltas are a very common feature of most landscapes.

The author remembers in the 'fifties travelling along the A861 through Glen Tarbert from Loch Linnhe to Loch Sunart. In those days, it was a single-track road with passing places. At the highest point, the road levelled out and, quite frankly, was a mess of stones and plant debris—clear evidence of recent flooding.

Unusually for those days, there was an interpretation board at the passing place, which explained that the stream coming down from the north (out of the Choire a'Chothruim) was called the Allt A'Chothruim, the Burn of the Balance. (Do you remember when shops had scales with the goods in a pan on one side and weights on the other? And it swung about until a balance was reached?)

Like the Nile, the burn would split and send its contents unpredictably, sometimes one way, sometimes the other and, in times of flood, sometimes both ways at once, causing havoc on the road.

In the 1960s, in an effort to improve communication and create local employment, the government introduced a Highland Counties Scheme, which sought to improve Highland roads in short stretches, using, wherever possible, local contractors and local labour. The road through Glen Tarbert was improved under this scheme. The opportunity was taken to clear up the problem at the watershed.

A new stretch of road was built further up the valley side and a deeper channel cut for the burn, so that all the water from the corrie was deflected west. The new bend in the river was reinforced with masonry from the old bridge and massive stone blocks from the hillsides.

As a result, the streams no longer roam freely but have been forced into conformity—in the interests of providing a high-speed link between Strontian and the rest of the United Kingdom.

The first recognised use of the word 'corrom' occurs in Charlesworth's *The Quaternary Era*, reading at pages 505 and 506 in Chapter XXV (Post-glacial readjustments), where he says:

U-valleys are being harmonised with present conditions…Cliffs have slumped to less bold and more stable slopes, and the U has been replaced by the V cross-section. Lateral streams have incised shallow clefts in the walls and faceted spurs, and small notches have been cut into the lips of hanging valleys…

Over steepened sides in favourable structures have been wasted by slips; slopes have crumbled and been encumbered with talus (some blocks exhibit glacial scratches on one side); and cones and deltas have been heaped up at the mouths of tributaries. Streams have built watershed deltas or 'corroms' on the passes to give rise to lakelets e.g. in the North-West Highlands of Scotland.

JB Sissons, in *The Evolution of Scotland's Scenery* (1967) (Edinburgh and London: Oliver and Boyd) is clearer, if less dramatic:

Quite frequently alluvial fans have been built out across the floors of channels by streams entering from their sides. These fans are sometimes referred to as 'corroms' from the Gaelic word, literally meaning, a 'balance', for the streams that built them (and, in some instances, that are still building them) may flow either way along the meltwater channel.

However, even by 1989, 'corrom', the Anglicised version of Chothruim, had not made it into the second edition of the *Oxford English Dictionary*.

It might be asked, 'What's all the fuss about?' An obscure word for an almost totally anonymous landscape feature, recognisable only to a handful of specialists. But there is another angle, the enormous feeling of satisfaction at recognising on the ground something one has only read about, the completion of a highly personal circle.

Charles Lyell (1797-1875), Scottish geologist, died a Baronet and was buried in Westminster Abbey. The best place for a Great Scot! He is remembered for Uniformitarianism ('the present is the key to the past'—no need for miracles); for dividing the geological record into time periods, mainly based on fossils; and for *Principles of Geology*.

Darwin took the *Principles* on his voyage in the *Beagle* and, for him, Lyell was 'the one man in Europe, whose opinion of the general truth of a longish argument'; (Darwin was) 'always most anxious to hear'.

Lyell was responsible for the introduction of at least two geological terms into the English language. In his chapter on *Causes of Earthquakes and Volcanos,* he describes 'the Geysers of Iceland', particularly the great Geyser. He devotes five pages to the geyser, its appearance and violence, the noise, the frequency of eruption and the surrounding deposits. He gives us a view of the crater and has a 'supposed section' of the subterranean reservoir and pipe of a geyser.

Fig 9:
View of the crater of the great Geyser in Iceland
(*Principles of Geology*)

Unfortunately, since Lyell's time, the underground geology has altered and the great Geyser is a shadow—and an irregular shadow—of its greatness.

However, Strockr nearby has taken over as the tourist attraction and has the great merit of erupting spectacularly every 8-10 minutes, engendering great satisfaction among the tourists, who are sure of getting their picture and moving on to the next stop.

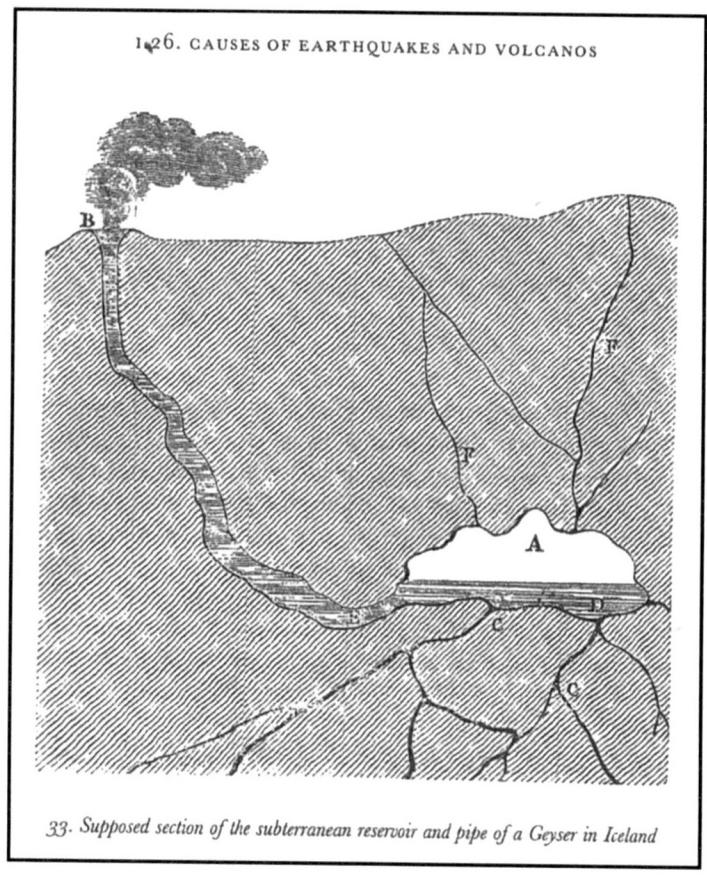

Fig 10:
Subterranean reservoir and pipe of a Geyser in Iceland
(*Principles of Geology*)

The area around the geyser is an unattractive muddle of smoking vents, mud pools, strangely coloured water and crusty deposits. We know it is just a work of Nature, of certain temperatures and pressures, of gases and chemicals, yet the whole place seems evil and malevolent. Rhynie—which we will visit later—must have been a little like this millions of years ago, when the Rhynie Chert was being formed.

For the author, however, there is the greatest satisfaction in not only seeing a wonder of nature, but of seeing for myself the original whose name has been given to the world. Completion is the word.

In his previous chapter, *Temple of Serapis,* Lyell rambles around the 'ring of fire' that is the Bay of Naples, investigating earthquakes and volcanic eruptions associated with Vesuvius, Pompeii, Herculaneum, the Flegrean Fields and Pozzuoli (which he called Puzzuoli), giving the dates of the various eruptions.

Pozzuoli is a remarkable place. Here Saint Peter and Saint Paul landed on their way to Rome. The so-called Temple of Serapis shows how the land here has gone up and down in recent times, and the sea has advanced and receded. (The frontispiece of the book is a woodcut of the 'Present state of the Temple of Serapis' and he has also a plan of the area and two sections; see Fig 11.)

On the way uphill, a Roman colosseum is still in daily use, and then one passes the fine villa that Sophia Loren bought for her parents. At the top of the hill, we come to what Lyell calls the Solfatara, where we descend into a former volcanic crater.

This is an uncomfortable place. The crater floor is more or less flat. One part has planted trees, a camp site and a centre with café, toilets and a shop. The rest of the floor is of volcanic ash, with no vegetation at all. The steep walls of the crater have some shrubby cover, and at the outer rim can be seen the suburban growth of Solfatara. At various points, there are, in Lyell's words, volcanic vents 'from which sulphur, sulphurous, watery and acid vapours and gases are emitted'.

These vents are the solfataras and simmer away ominously, filling the atmosphere with acrid fumes. As with the Icelandic geyser, the whole area is unsettling and even threatening.

On the floor at one point is a former Roman bathhouse, with notices warning us from going in. Last summer, one tourist ignored the warning and died.

Thanks to Lyell, solfatara has passed into the vocabulary of volcanology and examples are found all over the world, but there is a special frisson to be experienced when walking around the crater whose name has gone round the world and to find it is still fuming away.

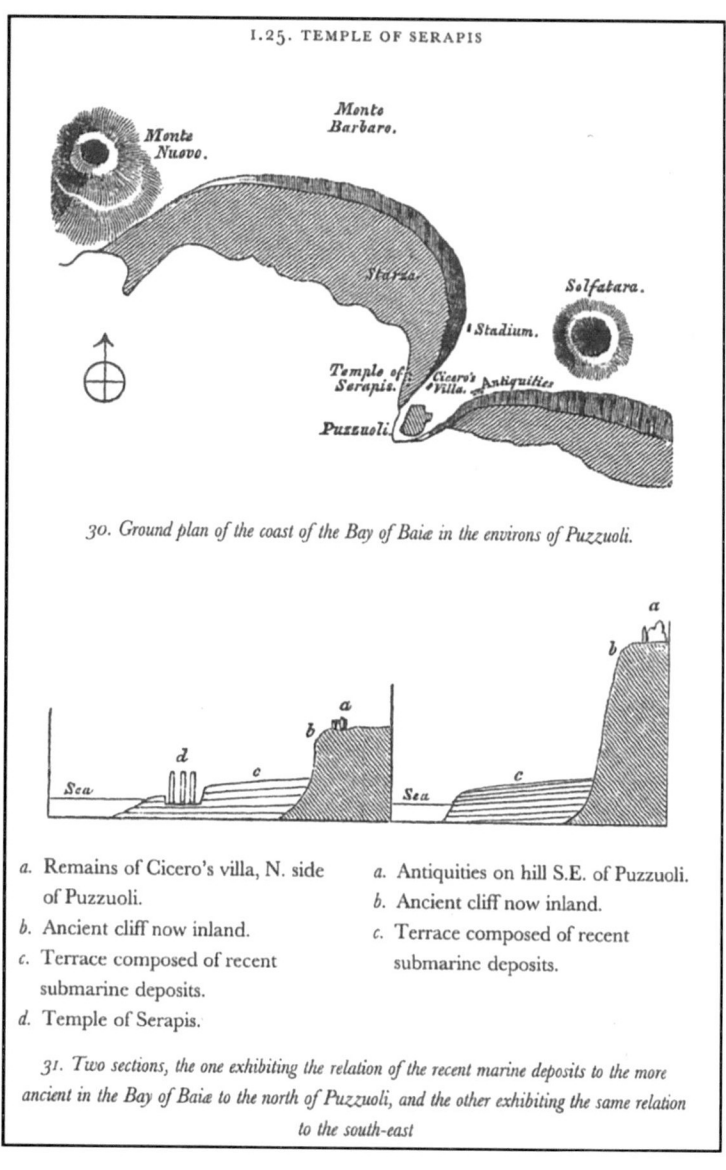

Fig 11:
Plan and sections in the environs of Puzzuoli
(*Principles of Geology*)

Scotland's corrom is not in the same class as geyser or solfatara, either as a natural phenomenon nor as a tourist attraction, but it has its own interest for a certain few!

The Trail

The pedant will question the status of Allt A'Chothruim, the Burn of the Balance, as an interesting place. Although, every day hundreds of drivers whizz over the burn, most are totally ignorant of its existence, far less its significance.

Also, it stretches credibility that any sane person would want to make the long journey here just for its own sake. Even though its inspection does not necessitate a detour. However, it is on the way to Strontian and is worth a few minutes.

From the Ardgour side of the Corran Ferry, the A861 follows the lochside south for 5 miles till, at Inversanda, it turns westwards and begins to climb Glen Tarbert. This is a typical U-shaped valley, the result of heavy glaciation. On either side are over steepened craggy hills. The valley floor is moderately flat, but is dotted with masses of ice-smoothed rock.

Big erratics help to break up the monotony. Going further up the glen, the floor is covered in hummocky moraine until, approaching the highest point of the road much of the valley floor flattens out quite remarkably.

Park at the cattle grid at the highest point, on what is clearly a new stretch of road. Up to the right (north) is the gullied Allt A'Chothruim, coming out of the Choire a'Chothruim of Garbh Bheinn (Rough Mountain). The first 200 yards or so are clearly an inland delta, with the stream crossing the hillside to be crossed by the new road bridge 100 yards below the highest point of the road. Coming down the eastern side of the delta can be seen the decayed course of another branch of the Allt A'Chothruim, heading off towards Loch Linnhe.

Turning round and looking down to the south, stretches of the old single-track can be seen, and beyond them, an extensive area of flat ground and indeterminate drainage. Beyond that again, we are on to the rocky slopes of Meall a'Choirein Luachraich, with a few young plantations at their foot.

Walking down to the new bridge, we note the sign:

Allt A'chothruim

From the bridge, we can see that massive engineering works have ensured that the burn turns a sharp corner and heads westwards towards Loch Sunart. I am sure that the good folk of Strontian have benefitted from the change—but for me, it is a pity to see the end of such an interesting, if little known, phenomenon.

Chapter Six

A Deep Subject
Dr William Mackie and Rhynie

Rhynie is a village in Aberdeenshire. The *Ordnance Gazetteer* of 1884, based on Sir Archibald Geikie's Geological Survey of 1878, dismissed the geology of the parish of Rhynie in four lines, yet, in 1912, Dr William Mackie, a medical practitioner and amateur geologist from Elgin, prowling around the drystane dykes of the countryside, found some unusual siliceous rocks. These we now call the Rhynie Chert.

Just as, near Siccar Point, James Hutton gave Sir James Hall the task of searching out the occasional piece of greywacke amongst the Old Red Sandstone boulders in the drystane dykes, and that led Hutton to decide that here was the area to look for what was to become his famous unconformity; similarly, in 1912, it was Mackie who found some unusual siliceous rocks in a drystane dyke at Rhynie.

As serious geologists—including amateurs—do, he made thin sections of the rock, examined these under the microscope and found perfectly preserved plant stems in great detail. ('Exquisite' is the word usually used to describe their condition.) If you think this was easy to do, look at Fig 14! Mackie realised the importance of his find and brought in the specialists, who soon realised that this was not a trivial find of merely local interest but something of the greatest importance in the earth's history!

Mackie's greatness came from taking his hobby to a high level, from carefully and systematically searching where others had just looked and passed on, from having the skills to prepare specimens for close observation, and perhaps, above all, from the generosity and maturity of spirit to recognise that his contribution should be turned over to the professionals, with their greater resources and influential networks.

A lesser man might have wanted to keep his secret to himself, or even to hawk it around and sell it to the highest bidder, but for Mackie, it was enough that his discovery was developed and revealed to the world as an early land-based community of plants and animals, together with bacteria and fungi. Some of these were 'the earliest colonisers of the land'. So this is a world-famous place, not just a local curiosity.

Mackie's greatness was immortalised when one of the plants discovered—*Asteroxylon mackiei*—was named after him!

My interest in Rhynie and its world status was aroused in Amsterdam, where De Hortus Botanicus is one of the great gardens in the world. It was founded in 1638 by the city to serve as a herb garden for doctors and apothecaries. (What was to become the Royal Botanic Garden Edinburgh was founded in 1670 while Kew was founded in 1759).

Hortus contains more than six thousand trees and plants, indigenous and from the tropics. The first collection in the 17th century was amassed through plants and seeds brought back by the Dutch East India Company (VOC). For example, a single coffee plant—*Coffea arabica*—in the Hortus collection was the parent for the entire coffee culture of Central and South America.

The VOC brought back two small potted oil palms from Mauritius. After six years, they produced seeds. These were propagated throughout Southeast Asia and became an important plantation cash crop in the Dutch East Indies, now Indonesia.

In 1987, the University of Amsterdam pulled out of its commitment to cover the garden's expenses and the future after three hundred and fifty years looked bleak. But a community of individual supporters rallied round and the Amsterdam City Council has also come in as a supporter. Nevertheless, the garden today shows the usual signs of underfunding—ageing buildings and poor garden maintenance.

A garden is, by definition, always changing. Although, it is quiet and peaceful and has many lovely plants, Hortus is not a pleasure garden, an urban paradise. It is a place of learning and of research. But Hortus has gone to meet and interest its public in a number of ways. Near the entrance buildings, the 1638 herb garden has been recreated.

Adjacent, in a fan-shaped arrangement, the Plant Kingdom is arranged physiologically, according to Linnaeus's system. This was based on observable characteristics, such as height, number and shape of flowers, leaves, etc.

Next is another fan-shaped arrangement of the Plant Kingdom, this time based on the new tool of taxonomy—plant DNA. There is plenty of interest in noting the similarities and differences between the two collections.

The garden now has a number of trails, designed to focus on specific themes, such as plants from the East Indies, and to spread visitors around the garden! One of these is an Evolution trail, and it was when following this, that I took the photograph, shown here as PLATE 4a.

At the time, I was attending an Extra-mural Introduction to Botany, so I proudly took my photo to the next meeting and shyly proffered it to the lecturer on the way out. 'What's this! This is impossible! Nobody's ever seen this! It's been extinct for millions of years!'

How right he was; what is on show in Amsterdam is a modern reconstruction of something that grew many millions of years ago. But why is it so important that it has a special place in one of the great botanic gardens of the world? And what has Rhynie, a douce little Aberdeenshire village, got to do with it?

We are all familiar with flint, a form of quartz which is found in nodules in much softer chalk and is tough enough to give a spark when struck by steel or to serve as tools for our ancestors. Less familiar may be chert, which is considered to be very similar in composition, but of lower quality—although, some varieties (like agate, opal and onyx) may be classed as semi-precious.

Essentially chert is a sedimentary rock of very fine silica particles. Sometimes silica-rich animal remains are consolidated. More often, silica-rich fluids penetrate and replace existing sediments which have been buried. In the case of Rhynie, surface deposits were saturated and transformed by these fluids.

The Rhynie Chert is one of the most interesting rocks in the world, and for good reason. A look at a good geological map of north-east Scotland shows a zone of tortured rocks, running north-eastwards from Braemar to the sea at Portsoy. From the Cambrian period onwards, there have been three major mountain-building episodes affecting Europe—the Caledonian (trending south-west to north-east across Scotland and Scandinavia), the Hercynian (Brittany, Massif Central, Rhine Highlands, etc.) and the Tertiary (Pyrenees, Alps, Carpathians, Apennines, etc.).

Along the area where Rhynie now is, was an inferno of volcanic, geyser and hot pool activity, with silica-rich (sinter) cones being thrown up and destroyed.

Sir Charles Lyell (1797-1876) first propounded that 'the present is the key to the past' and if, today, we wanted to observe what the Rhynie area was undergoing 400 million years ago, it would be necessary to visit Yellowstone in the United States, Rotorua in New Zealand, or Iceland.

At the same time (about 416 million years ago) as these violent ongoings, some of the earliest plants and animals were beginning to colonise the land. As the layers of sinter built up, this living material was incorporated into the siliceous deposits, the organic structures were replaced by minerals, and eventually converted into chert.

What makes Rhynie special is, firstly, this is the oldest hot spring system known anywhere in the world where surface features, such as geyser vents, are preserved. Secondly, the preservation of the fossil plants and animals is absolutely perfect, which enables the precise analysis and identification of an early land-based community of plants and animals, together with bacteria and fungi. Thirdly, some of these were 'the earliest colonisers of the land'. So this is a world-famous place.

Incredible though it may seem, the tiniest detail, external and internal, of these little creatures can be studied and measured 400 million years later, despite countless floods, earthquakes and the assault of wind and water.

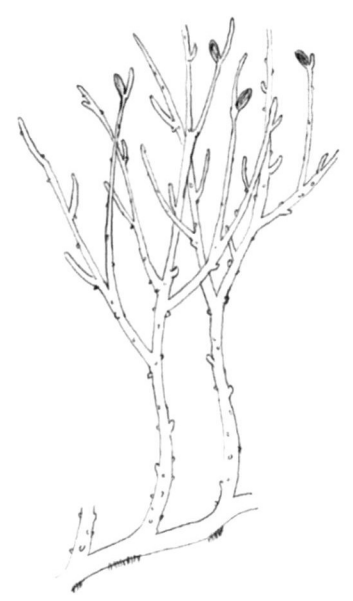

Fig 12:
Reconstruction of *Rhynia Gwynne-vaughanii*
(University of Aberdeen)

For example, *Rhynia gwynne-vaughanii* (Dame Helen Gwynne-Vaughan, 1870-1967; botany professor, Birkbeck College, 1921-44; 1917-19, Controller of Women's Army Auxiliary Corps and Commandant of Women's Royal Air Force; 1930, chaired the Girl Guides' Sixth World Conference) is known only from the Rhynie Chert, but six other named higher land plants have been identified.

At least 15 (the work goes on) species of land-living and freshwater arthropods—spider-like creatures and primitive insects—have been found here, including 'the oldest fossil insect in the world'. The oldest known arthropod fossils in the world are named, appropriately, *Rhyniella* and *Rhynieognatha.*

The fossil-bearing chert extends for about 100 metres and is buried under at least 1 metre of later deposits. Trenches were cut into the field between 1917 and 1921, and Dr Robert Kidston and Professor William Lang worked furiously, finding new plant fossils and publishing their results. The next wave of discovery came with Dr Alexander Lyon in the late 1950s, who collected new material by further trenching from 1963-71.

Lyon also bought the fields overlying the deposits and gifted them to Scottish Natural Heritage, thus ensuring their interdiction to commercial fossil-hunters. The evolution of the site was further unravelled from 1980 by the University of Münster and from 1987 by Aberdeen University. Cores and further trenching provided more knowledge in depth, and also discovered the 'Windyfield chert' 700 metres from the Rhynie outcrop.

Science never stands still. Until recently, the Rhynie Chert was the only deposit of its kind known from the geological record but something similar has now been discovered in Argentina, and it is likely that the forces which created the Rhynie deposits left traces in other locations with a similar geological history.

I have to confess to a feeling of complete inadequacy when considering these matters of geological time. I just cannot get hold of the meaning of the Devonian or Old Red Sandstone period 410 million years ago, or of the slow drift of what was to become Scotland from near the South Pole to its present location, drifting away from North America. I can easily understand poor Lapworth, who lost his wits by looking so far into the abyss of time.

Nor can I cope with the numbers and the odds that—so far as we know—some of the very first plants and arthropods to make it on to the land, lay there in wait to be discovered by a Scottish doctor in his spare time.

Rhynie is unique in being 'weel-kent' to the practitioners of three disciplines—Botany, Zoology and Geology—but the eager tourist is in for a disappointment if he or she arrives, primed for photography, to record this unique location. All he will find is a small field outside the village (PLATE 4b). But the work goes on.

When the field is ploughed, fossil-bearing chert stones may be turned up. Occasionally, a bore is drilled into the bedrock, bringing up cores without disturbing the surface cover.

But Rhynie is all about stones, other stones, not just the Rhynie Chert. Groome records that, in the 1880s, there were, in the parish:

...cairns, tumuli, several standing stones (four of them sculptured and very good of their kind), and remains of a large vitrified fort...with walls more than 10 feet thick.

The Ordnance Survey 25-inch map of 1895 shows, within the confines of the village: Part of Sculptured Stone found 1808, Sculptured Stone found 1803, Sculptured Stones found 1834, Sculptured Stones found 1836, Standing Stones, Urns found, Human Remains found. By 1978, the number of Pictish symbol stones found at Rhynie had gone up to eight.

On the Revised Explorer map of 2002, within 2Km of the village were: the Craw Stane and another Symbol Stone, the remains of three Stone Circles and a Standing Stone on the Hill of Noth. In 1978, a splendid symbol stone 2 metres high was turned up by the plough just outside Rhynie. Near the Craw Stane, forming a kind of gateway, it was said to be of gabbro (an igneous rock usually associated with the Cuillin of Skye). 'Rhynie Man' is full-size, with turned up pointed shoes, a kilt, tunic or skirt, and carries an axe over his shoulder.

With just a few lines cut into the stone, his head is a beautiful cartoon, with an unforgettable profile. Rhynie Man was obviously a person of some importance—possibly the Celtic god Esus—and is now appropriately to be found in the entrance to the Aberdeenshire Council offices in Aberdeen, the headquarters of today's Northern Pictland.

Rhynie clearly had some considerable importance in man's early days in the vicinity.

Aberdeenshire still shows traces of when it was part of Northern Pictland. There are place-names like Pitfour, Pitgaveny, Pitlurg, Pittodrie, Pitsligo. The sculptured stones of Rhynie and dozens of other places are survivals of Pictland.

The older generation still greet each other with 'Aye, aye min. Fit like' and their dialogues are laden with *fit*(what) and *fitever* (whatever), *fat*(what) and *foo*(who), *fan*(when) and *fanever*(whenever), *fae* (from) and *fas* (whose, as in the famous saying of Jamie Fleeman, the Laird of Udny's fool to the supercilious courtier—'Ah'm the Laird o' Udny's feel. Fas feel are 'ee?').

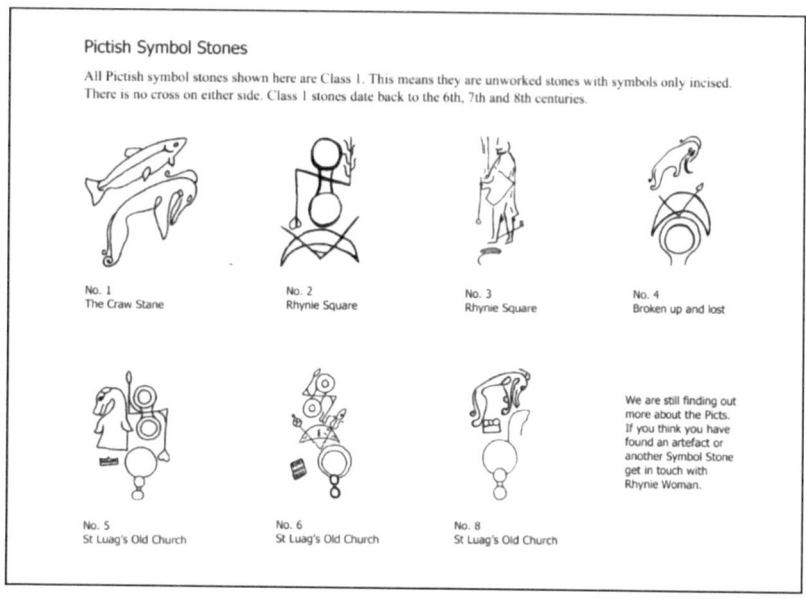

Fig 13:
Rhynie's Pictish Symbol Stones
(Anne Murray, Rhynie Walks, Rhynie Woman)

The Rev Alexander Mackay, Free Church minister of Rhynie from 1844 to 1867, is not exactly a 'weel-kent' figure—but his life was not quite without interest. Mackay, born in Thurso in 1816, was inducted to the charge one year after the Disruption, when a mass walkout from the General Assembly of the Church of Scotland reformed and revitalised Presbyterianism in Scotland. Until 1861, services were held in 'a wooden construction hastily erected outside the parish'.

In 1867, he was persuaded to take early retirement as 'this once large and flourishing congregation (was) now so broken up and scattered…'. He was accused of 'unedifying preaching…imprudent conduct, and giving his time to other pursuits'.

Although Darwin's *The Origin of Species* had been published in 1865, Mackay seemed to have found a satisfactory position in the evolution debate, 'harmonising the workings of the natural realm with biblical revelation'. But he had certainly caught the natural history bug, involving his young son in the exploration of the area, networking with geologists, the Astronomer Royal, and other Royal Geographical Society members. He was on one of the committees for the 1869 British Association at Aberdeen.

He hosted at Rhynie Sir Roderick Murchison, Director-General of the British Geological Survey and President of the RGS. In 1861, he published a highly successful *Manual of Modern Geography* and in 1865 Aberdeen University awarded him an LID for services to geography. After so much intellectual activity, the exegesis of the Scriptures to the small farmers and crofters in 'the Dead Sea of Strathbogie' must have seemed a doleful chore.

Mackay moved to Edinburgh, then the Isle of Wight and proceeded to churn out many successful books combining religion, Geography and education. The most user-friendly was *Rhyming Geography for little boys and girls* (1873). It included 'geographical verses', like this one, to the Psalm tune St Andrews:

East Lothian next, or Haddington
For cornfairs widely known,
Has coal and limestone, while the soil
Consists of rich clay loam.

One of Mackay's sons, Alexander Murdoch Mackay (1848-90), became an engineering missionary for the Church Missionary Society, was known as 'Mackay of Uganda' and acted as a source for his father to update his textbooks.

So strange it is to think of this fellow searching for truth in the Bible and among the rocks and hedgerows while, under his feet, quietly lay such tiny fragments of evidence he could never have dreamed of.

If Rhynie is 'weel-kent' at all, it is not for its maverick minister, its fossils or its Pictish echoes but for its notoriety at the hands of 'Scotland the What?', a sophisticated Doric cabaret trio who flourished in the north-east and beyond from 1969 till 1995—described by themselves with false modesty as 'three semi-literate Scots taking an irreverent look at their country's institutions'.

Witty sketches in the Doric and their own sharp songs had a great following in their own territory, yet their material was so universal—the corrupt councillor, the naïve but cunning country bumpkin, the pretentious politician, the man who 'kent your faither'—that they could tour worldwide and still fill the house. Their strip-cartoon, *Councillor Swick* (Swick in the Doric means Cheat) ran regularly in *Leopard: The Magazine for North-East Scotland*, published in Pictish-sounding Pitcaple.

For them, Rhynie—40 miles from Aberdeen, with its oil, university and theatres—embodied remoteness and backwardness, as in: 'We get an awfu lot o' sna' in that bottom field...in A-a-ugust!' In one of their sketches, there is a mention of the Station Hotel at Rhynie, the joke being that there is no railway station at Rhynie, '...but they were aye hopin' for one'.

The Trail

The purpose of these trails is to help the interested reader to go out and check for oneself the evidence put forward by the author. But how can we have a Rhynie trail when the evidence is either underground or occasionally dug up by the plough, or in Edinburgh or Aberdeen?

Would any sane person want to make the long journey to Rhynie on the off-chance of making a discovery where, for a century, experts have repeatedly gone over the same ground, digging the occasional trench, combing the dykes and following the plough like seagulls? And would any such find be recognised as such by the layman?

But if we think of Stones in the Landscape as a subject, it is possible to set up a series of interesting visits which have some sort of cohesion and relate to the Aberdeenshire area—where there is no shortage of stones. So we can go to Rhynie to see the village as a case study of one kind of traditional settlement in a landscape of stones, in which one, quite rare, stone, is of world-wide interest.

So our Rhynie Trail is really a Sermon in Stones.

My quest began in Amsterdam, but to start, we need to go no further than Edinburgh.

1. If we want to see what Rhynia and the rest looked like, we must go to the **Royal Museum of Scotland** in Edinburgh, where we will find two fine examples of the **Rhynie Chert**. On Level 3 of the old RMS is the **Restless Earth Gallery,** and there, modestly as part of a display of **First Life Forms**, is a large polished block, measuring c750 x 300 x 230 mm.

Fig 14:
First Life Forms in Rhynie Chert
(Royal Museum of Scotland)

The polished face shows a hotchpotch of nodules and lines in several shades of grey, brown and black. There are definite layers twisting across the face, but the general impression is of apparently random patches. With the eye of faith, an expert can, perhaps, discern lines which might be plant stems cutting across the layers.

The label says:

Rhynie Chert preserves some of the first life forms to colonise the land. Within this silica-rich rock are at least 15 species of land-living and freshwater arthropods, including spider-like creatures and primitive insects. There are also seven species of primitive plants…This ecosystem developed 400-412 million years ago when Scotland had many volcanos and hot springs.

Upstairs now to Level 5 and the Life Evolves section. Here there is a large case of Evidence for Evolution.

Its main feature is a large grid. Reading from right to left is a time-scale from the Devonian to the Present. Down the right-hand side are:

Horseshoe crabs
Ammonoids
Sea urchins
Insects

Dating from between 416 and 359 million years ago, in the Insect box, there is a small plaque (c300 mm square) labelled 'Rhynie Chert—source of earliest fossil insects'. (To put it into context, insect evolution is shown to have resulted in models of Hymenoptera [bees, wasps, ants, etc.], Coleoptera [beetles, weevils, etc.], and Orthoptera [crickets, locusts, grasshoppers, etc.].)

Like the big sample downstairs, this plaque seems at first sight to be a random smattering of brown, grey and black particles, but there is a horizontal banding and one yellowish worm-like vertical, about 50mm long, cuts through the grain of the mass.

Off we go now, northwards to Aberdeenshire, to Mossat Toll, where the A944 meets the A97. A mile north, one pulls into a rather nice little car park for about twenty vehicles. There are pedestrian signposts to 'Sculpture Walk' (which is marked on the Ordnance Survey map) and a metal frame for an information board, but no board!

This must be Aberdeenshire's second-best secret (after Rhynia). When one wanders around, one finds no sculptures, only a rather fine esker lined with mature beeches.

This is not the place to start the trail. One must go a couple of hundred yards, past the school, to find a large metal sculpture by the roadside. Below it, and running along parallel with the road, is the trail. Here are displayed some of the substantial sculptures created at the other end of the village of Lumsden.

On my visit, there were several metal sculptures and two sizeable shaped and trimmed blocks of granite, but the display varies as most of the works are commissioned and go off to their final destinations.

When one gets back to the car, one notes that the Ordnance Survey have located the star for the Walk on the wrong side of the school. Not a good start.

2. Continue through **Lumsden,** a planned stone village, with a central square. In Aberdeenshire were about 84 planned villages, recognised by their rectangular streets of modest cottages of local stone, built right up to the road, but with decent plots of land behind. Often the central focus was The Square, which was and still is in Lumsden a square of grass, but could also be a rectangle (Rhynie), a triangle (Inverurie) or an amorphous shape, as in Meigle in Angus.

Leaving Lumsden, almost the last buildings on the right are those of the Scottish Sculpture Workshop. Dating from 1979, it was the first sculpture-specific artist workshop to be developed in the UK, offering the time, space, support and facilities to artists from all backgrounds to develop their practice, with an emphasis on experimentation and exploration of sculpture within the expanded field, locale within a globalised society.

The core programme of SSW is based around the facilitation of artist residencies, the delivery of projects and the provision of facilities, as well as offering open access to workshops for all.

Approaching Rhynie, on the right, on top of a small hill, can be seen the Craw Stane, which can be approached from the road, but is kept by me for the last point in my tour of Rhynie.

3. **Rhynie**—note the planned stone village with one straight main street, a mixture of single-storey cottages and two-storey houses, with the occasional later additions, incomplete cross-streets and modern accretions. The Square is a public garden sweeping down to the tidy Gothic parish church (Church of Scotland—'The Auld Kirk') with a fine belltower/steeple on its north-east corner.

   Granite is a rather intractable building material, so the lintels, sills, door and window frames are cut from attractive sandstone, probably from the Moray coast.

Across the road, just inside the garden, are two symbol stones, nos 2 and 3, which have been located here from their original situations. Their symbols (see Fig 13) are not at all clear.

4. Beside the **church,** we can pick up an excellent guide to Rhynie Walks, produced by Rhynie Woman, an arts collective devoted to enhancing the community. Across the road, the 1895 map shows the school. It is still there, of course, functioning in its original stone building. Behind the church, the 'Market Stance' of 1895 has become a green space with a football pitch with one floodlight, picnic benches and a safe kiddies' play area.

   No markets in a wee place like Rhynie in the 21st century! Follow the road, now called Eassie Road. Just before the bridge was the Poorhouse, set in a neat garden, well away from the village. Now we have a little forest, and modern bungalows have taken over the remaining area.

5. Cross the Bridge of Easaiche and look up to the fields, half-right. Proceed up the road till you come to a point where a minor road breaks off, back up the hill. This road is very narrow and has only one passing-place, so proceed with care till it flattens out and one can look back down to the field, the little bridge and Rhynie.

This is the **Windyfield**, a SSSI (Site of Special Scientific Interest) and the location which has caused all the fuss. Who knows what mysteries remain undiscovered below the very ordinary looking surface?

Now it is back down to the village, turning left just before the school.

6. On the 1895 map, the village is called Muir of Rhynie and the area before us was divided into 1.2-acre plots running back from the houses on Main Street. Going in to **Richmond Gardens,** we find blocks of local authority houses in traditional style, using reconstituted granite, and arranged around a central green space.

   Going on to Richmond Terrace, on the right is the Rhynie Community Centre and the large playground behind the school. On the left are 4-in-a-block council houses. Turning left along Richmond Avenue, on the right are the truncated plots of the Main Street houses, with many new sheds, greenhouses, etc. Plot 70 is conspicuous with two long, low, stone buildings from 'the old days'—byres for cattle.

This is Gordon country, so why is this a Richmond estate? The 5th Duke of Gordon died in 1836, when the Dukedom became extinct. Most of the Gordon estates passed to the son of the 5th Duke's eldest sister, the 5th Duke of Richmond, of Goodwood House in Sussex.

His son, the 6th Duke of Richmond was created Duke of Gordon, of Gordon Castle in Scotland, and Earl of Kinrara in the County of Inverness. The present title-holder is Charles Gordon-Lennox, 11th Duke of Richmond, 11th Duke of Lennox, 11th Duke of Aubigny, 6th Duke of Gordon, founder of the Goodwood Festival of Speed and the Goodwood Revival.

7. Now turn on to the main road and prepare to walk back to The Square. In 1895, there were four places of worship in Rhynie and, amazingly in our secular age, these buildings can still be seen. At the north end of the village, the **Congregational Chapel** (or 'Congie Kirk') is still to be found, although it has seen better days.

The style is Utilitarian Early English. Neat sandstone is the building material. At the south end, the roof is sagging and the masonry is cracking. The lower halves of the windows are covered over, and all the openings of the little hall are filled with concrete blocks.

Its future as a church is very much in doubt but Rhynie Woman, who have a Rhynie Archive, and the Rhynie Charitable Trust have plans to renovate the building and give it a new life with stories, artefacts and found objects. Rhynie Man would, of course, be brought back from Aberdeen.

8. Head back to The Square, turn left at Bogie Terrace, follow Bogie Road, and cross the Bridge of Bogie. (The local river is the Water of Bogie and the district is Strathbogie). Up on the right is **St Mary's Auchindoir**, a simple Early English 'Piskie Kirk' of the Scottish Episcopal Church, built in 1859, extended in 1883, and with a service on the first Sunday of every month.

9. Back to **The Square**, turn left. Note the unroofed building where renovation seems to have been halted and behind it, tucked in unobtrusively, the former Free Church of Scotland ('Free Kirk') of 1851. These were the church and manse of the Rev Alexander Mackay until he was persuaded to leave in 1867.

Latterly, this was the home of Dr Alexander Lyon, who loved Rhynie, bought the 'fossil field' and donated it to the Scottish Natural Heritage, thus ensuring its suitable management.

10. Turn uphill and take the fork to **St Luag's Old Church and Cemetery**. In the car park, look at what looks like, at a distance, a broken old tool shed. Closer inspection reveals three stones with the characteristic Pictish carvings. Then we notice that we missed a modern slab headed 'The Stone Circle' and the message—Rhynie Pictish Symbol Stones.
11. Climb the path outside the cemetery wall and, near the top, cross the grass field to **The Craw Stane** (PLATE 5a). Where it is on the hill, it looks over the lower land around Rhynie and across to Tap o' Noth (563 metres and Iron Age fort). Incised on the south side are a salmon, and what I think of as a Pictish elephant, but the experts call the Pictish Beast.

This must have been a very special place. Close by, in 1978, Rhynie Man was found by local farmers, Gavin and Kenneth Alston, when ploughing. In 2011, archaeologists uncovered a substantial fortified settlement. It seems that the Craw Stane stood at the inner entrance to a stronghold which had two ditched ramparts and an outer palisade with an annexe to the west.

Among the finds were fragments of a late Roman amphora, the only known example of a Roman amphora from Eastern Britain dating to the post-Roman period. This suggests not only trade links with the Mediterranean but that the residents must have been something quite special.

It is now recognised that the site must have been a special place of Pictish power or ritual, and is now being popularly described as 'a Pictish palace'. And Rhynie is thought to translate as 'A Very Royal Place'!

The stones at Rhynie are all Class 1, meaning that they are pre-Christian. Very little is known about the Picts, their language, their customs, their beliefs. But up here at the Craw Stane, it is easy to imagine a Pictish king or princeling strutting about his stronghold, monarch of all he surveys below.

Did he wonder at how it all happened? Who created this? Who came before him and his ancestors? What is to happen when we die? He would have found it difficult to accept that—so many millions of years before—this land would have been so different.

12. And now it's back to Rhynie, to Mossat Toll and the A944—destination Aberdeen. An hour's drive takes us to the Westhill and Kingswells area, which is quite appalling. Partly as a result of the oil boom, these settlements have expanded enormously in what seems a totally uncontrolled fashion. New roads and roundabouts have appeared faster than they can be mapped, and there is a plethora of huge factory sheds and research and finance centres.

At one of the many roundabouts, you will see a ring road to Bucksburn going off to the left. Follow this to a set of traffic lights. Turn left, park at a newly created viewpoint, walk to the edge and look down the hill.

In Scotland, the Age of Enlightenment was also the Age of Improvement. The old rural landscape was transformed, first by clearing the land of stones which were used to build dykes around the newly-created fields. Dr Francis Edmond, as an improver, was slow off the mark in that it was only in 1850, that he acquired the Kingswells estate and began its improvement.

The result was a **consumption dyke** which has been preserved as an Ancient Monument. It measures 440 metres by 10 metres and is 2 metres high (PLATE 5b) There are steps at each end, with a paved path along the top and a water-bay in the middle. The dykes around Rhynie were certainly substantial but not spectacular, like this. There are smaller consumption dykes on the former estate while *Aberdeenshire Sites and Monuments* lists 117 such **consumption dykes**.

This is one of the most impressive monuments of agricultural improvement in the north-east. Only by walking along the central path, can it become clear to anyone the immense amount of labour required to gather the cyclopean boulders and construct the dyke. Understandably, it has become an object of local pride, and its maintenance has been supported by Historic Scotland, Aberdeen Countryside Project and Aberdeen City Council (the dyke's owner).

Weeds and rubbish were cleared away by pupils from the nearby Hazlehead School, under the supervision of the City of Aberdeen Archaeology Section. Drum Property Group Ltd proposed 'redevelopment ' of the adjacent farmland, which would have debased the monumental simplicity of the dyke, but have been thwarted so far.

13. For the last stop on the Trail, go back to the roundabout, turn left along the A944 again. In Aberdeen, it becomes the Lang Stracht, cross the

ring road of Anderson Drive, to Westburn Road. Woodhill House, Aberdeenshire Council's headquarters, is the two massive concrete bunkers on the left.

In the reception area, you will find **Rhynie Man**, almost cartoon-like, over a metre high, beautifully carved and carrying an axe. Unfortunately, the carving on Class I stones does not photograph easily, but is absolutely clear to every visitor to the offices.

As *Undiscovered Scotland* says:

Why it was felt appropriate to house him in a building with such ill-signed and inadequate visitor parking is unclear, but it takes a little effort to find many of the best of Scotland's Pictish stones, and in that much at least, Rhynie Man is no exception.

In every other way, however, Rhynie Man is very unusual indeed. Very few carvings of figures have been found dating back to the Pictish period (between the 500s and the 800s).

...The absence of even a vague idea of a date makes it very difficult to agree what the stone actually depicts. But there is no shortage of theories.

Undiscovered Scotland charitably does not take exception to the building itself, as it might have done. Woodhill House is really an extreme example of concrete civic brutality, and one wonders whether it is a suitable location for such a precious relic from the past. The City of Aberdeen is well enough known, but the country around—Aberdeenshire—may have an image problem. Having Rhynie Man in such a place with a heavy footfall, may well contribute to a sense of place and give ordinary people some sense of pride in their region.

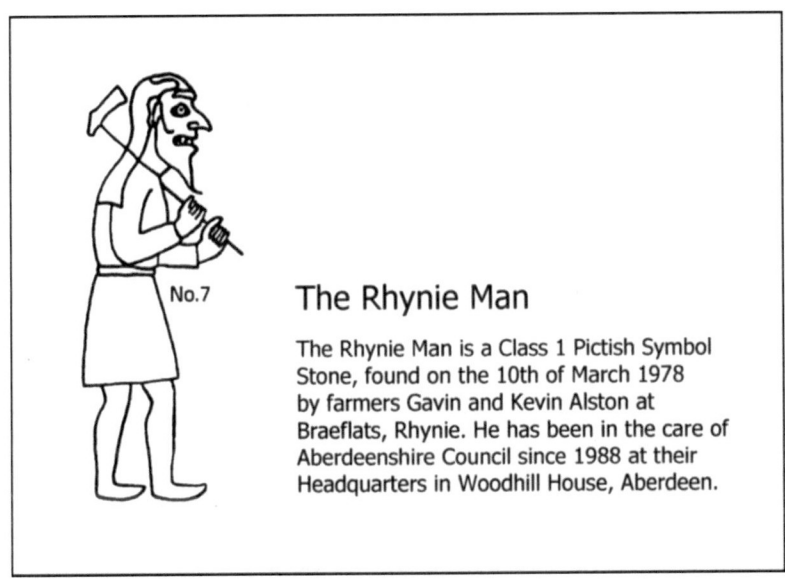

Fig 15:
The Rhynie Man
(Anne Murray, Rhynie Walks, Rhynie Woman)

On the other hand, the Greeks are demanding that we give them back the Elgin Marbles, while the Aboriginal people of Australia and New Zealand are seeking the return of the sacred relics of their ancestors. Surely, the Rhynie folk should have their forebear back in their midst? There is always tension between the two forces, the need to be accessible to a wide public, to have expert interpretation, good security and storage conditions, and the desire to have our own heritage beside us, accessible to all the bairns.

It will be interesting to see how this situation pans out.

Chapter Seven

An Imaginary Place?
Sir James Barrie and Thrums

Once, bumbling about San Francisco, I came across a little square in which was a modest memorial with a sailing ship. It recorded that Robert Louis Stevenson spent six months there from December 1879, returning in 1888, to pick up the yacht *Casco,* in which he sailed off to Samoa and his last home. So far from his 'Hills of Home', I was set wondering about the nature of greatness in authorship, before the days of literary prizes and internet lists.

What makes an author great? It is certainly not output. John Creasey (1908-1973) was immensely prolific and very popular. He wrote over 600 novels under 28 pseudonyms, but would have been the last person to think of himself as a great novelist. On the other hand, Jane Austen (1775-1817) had only four of her romantic novels published in her lifetime (and two published posthumously), but is unquestionably a great novelist and the basis for a raft of films, videos, copies and pastiches. Why?

The good Sir Walter Scott summed her up:
The Big Bow-Wow strain I can do myself like any now going; but the exquisite touch, which renders ordinary commonplace things and characters interesting, from the truth of the description and the sentiment, is denied to me.

>Kipling put her in context:
>Jane went to Paradise:
>>That was only fair,
>
>Good Sir Walter met her first,
>>And led her up the stair.
>
>Henry and Tobias,
>>And Miguel of Spain,
>
>Stood with Shakespeare at the top
>>To welcome Jane.

Miguel was, of course, Miguel Cervantes, creator of noble Don Quixote and his cowardly servant, Sancho Panza. He displays another kind of greatness as he created an immortal character known to millions who have never opened his book, and who unknowingly use words like 'quixotic' or phrases like 'tilting at windmills'.

It is a remarkable thing that, in one decade of the 19th century, three Scotsmen were born whose fame would resonate around the world and down through the ages, not only from the volume and quality of their work, but from at least one unforgettable creation each. R. L. S. (b 1854) gave us the *Hispaniola, Treasure Island* and its treasure map, pirates and Long John Silver—and they have been perpetuated in over 50 film and TV versions and over 24 major stage and radio adaptations.

They have inspired over 20 substantial sequels and prequels by lesser writers, and the stereotype of the one-legged charmer/villain with a parrot on his shoulder has passed into our collective psyche.

A few yards east of his birthplace in Picardy Place, Edinburgh was, until it was removed to make way for a bigger traffic island, a fine statue of Conan Doyle's (b 1859) immortal creation, Sherlock Holmes—hero of 4 novels and 56 short stories, revered by at least 250 societies worldwide and model for a century of detective writers. Guinness World Records has listed Holmes as the 'most portrayed movie character', with more than 70 actors playing the part in over 200 films, starting with his first appearance in the 1900 Mutoscope film, *Sherlock Holmes Baffled*.

'Elementary', 'a three-pipe problem', 'you know my methods', 'Elementary, my dear Watson' have all passed into the vocabulary of the educated, while *The Curious Incident of the Dog in the Night-time* has even made it to become an award-winning first novel by Mark Haddon (in 2003), adapted for the National Theatre in 2012.

Peter Pan was a wonderful creation who seems to be immortal. Even in the 21st century, our sophisticated and precocious children will give themselves up to the sentimentality of 'Do you believe in fairies? If you believe, clap your hands' yet again. And *Peter Pan: The Never-ending Story* is packing them in on its World Arena Tour.

James Barrie (b 1860), especially through *Peter Pan*, turns up in the oddest places, even today. In a recent flight from Berlin, I found in a seat pocket a paperback version of Barrie's masterpiece. It had not been left by an earlier passenger but was labelled 'Easy Jet Book Club—I live in the seat pocket. Please don't take me away'.

How clever, to ensure a good read on a tedious journey! The design was obviously aimed at children, but not patronisingly. After the main text, there was an author file of 14 pages which provided an introduction to 'lit crit'.

The hallmark of a great literary creation is whether it can stand up to adaptation, parody and mockery. Mischief Theatre—'an anarchic bunch of actors and writers'—certainly demonstrated this with their *Peter Pan Goes Wrong*. The Cornley Polytechnic Drama Society and their starry narrator (David Suchet—celebrated for his portrayal of Hercule Poirot) put on a show that is 'equally impressive and hilarious'.

Technical hitches and fluffed lines abound and 'are all held together with admirable precision and comic timing'. Barrie would have been proud of them!

Poor Peter has even made his way into the sordid world of Westminster politics. On a Friday in November 2015, a succession of Conservative MPs could be heard droning away at length on the merits of Peter Pan and how Wendy had formed their characters. The piece of legislation before them was a bill to confirm the rights to Peter Pan to the Great Ormond Street Hospital Trust—a non-controversial measure which could have been passed on the nod.

The filibustering 'debate' was merely a clever wheeze to talk out the Off-Patent Drugs Bill, which would have made cheap, existing medicines available to patients with a number of different conditions—not perhaps a wheeze that would have pleased Barrie.

Owing a lot to *Treasure Island,* Sir James Matthew Barrie (b 1860) cleverly manipulated the emotions of young and old with his invention of Peter Pan, Wendy, The Lost Boys, Neverland and the villainous Captain Hook. 'To die will be an awfully big adventure' is an awfully big idea to introduce to young minds. But this great work did not come out of the blue, Barrie could have been writing of himself when he wrote in *What Every Woman Knows*: 'There are few more impressive sights in the world than a Scotsman on the make'.

Barrie could be said to have ascended to the summit of Society's greasy pole when, in 1918, he took on a secretary who could neither take shorthand nor type. Lady Cynthia Asquith had, however, other talents. A daughter of the Earl of Wemyss and daughter-in-law of a former prime minister, she mixed with such as D. H. Lawrence and L. P. Hartley (*The Go-between*) and wrote novels, ghost stories and a biography of the Duchess of York (who later was to become Queen Elizabeth, then Queen Elizabeth, the Queen Mother).

Barrie left the bulk of his estate—minus the Peter Pan works—to Lady Cynthia.

The Order of Merit was founded by Edward VII in 1902. It is claimed as 'the pinnacle of the British honours system'. Only twenty-four individuals can be in the Order at any one time, and it is 'quite possibly the most prestigious honour one can receive on planet Earth'. James Barrie was already a Baronet when he was made OM in 1922. Not bad for one of a handloom weaver's family of ten from a little Angus town.

He 'gratefully acknowledged but graciously declined' the offer of burial in the Poets' Corner of Westminster Abbey, preferring to be buried 'where his heart lay'—among his ain folk in the town of his birth.

We are all familiar with the role of the cotton industry in the Industrial Revolution, how a wave of inventions resulted in the growth of huge spinning mills dependent on water power, in Lancashire and Derbyshire especially in England, and in Scotland at New Lanark, using the Falls of Clyde, and Stanley (on the Tay). Weaving was done on handlooms in the home but was organised, first on the 'putting out system' led by local merchants.

Then the weavers were brought together, under control, into 'manufactories', from which it was just a short step to bringing in new machinery, initially water-driven, then driven by the more reliable steam power, in huge spinning and weaving mills.

In eastern Scotland, particularly in Fife, Perthshire and Angus, flax was grown (and imported) to make linen. Flax was less tractable than cotton, so that the mechanisation of the linen industry lagged behind cotton. This had the result that times for the flax spinners and weavers were harder, although linen (and imported jute) took a long time to die. In Barrie's time in his home town:
Recently…two large power-loom factories have been erected. The weavers, in some years, particularly in 1826 and 1841, suffered severely from a great fall in wages; and often had to struggle with poverty and privation; but they have manfully breasted every difficulty, and are admitted throughout the county to be expert and skilful operatives.

In Barrie's words:
Another era had dawned…the daughter, till now but a knitter of stockings, became the breadwinner, he who had been the breadwinner sat down to the

knitting of stockings: what had been yesterday a nest of weavers was to-day a town of girls.

Barrie was born in The Tenements on the Brechin Road. His father was a handloom weaver, but not one of the poorest. The weavers were regarded as the intelligentsia of their day—'literate, numerate and articulate, and pretty political animals to boot'. His loom and yarn store were in a room on the ground floor. About 1868, he moved to another loom shop rented from his neighbour and the former loom shop became a parlour.

'If you can't beat them, join them'—David Barrie was forced into becoming a book-keeper in a linen factory in nearby Forfar, and then took up the post of chief confidential clerk in the very factory that had put him out of business.

Presbyterianism in Scotland was characterised by free-thinking and a deep-rooted suspicion of any authority other than the Bible. Most Scottish burghs in the late 19th century displayed 'three Kirks'—the 'Auld Kirk', the Church of Scotland parish church, the 'Free Kirk', dating from the Disruption of 1843, and the 'UP Kirk', the United Presbyterian Church, the coming together of small churches (the Auld Licht Burghers, the Auld Licht Anti-Burghers, the New Licht Burghers, the New Licht Anti-Burghers), which had seceded on various points of doctrine, which seem inconsequential to our modern eyes.

In Scotland generally, the UPs were prosperous and well-educated. They had the best churches because they could pay for the best architects.

In Barrie's hometown—full of disputatious weavers—there were two Church of Scotland churches, two Free Churches and two UP churches, as well as a United Original Secession Church and St Mary's Episcopal church.

Those who teach creative writing tell us that we must write from our own experience and Barrie was a master at this. *The Scotsman,* in reviewing *A Window in Thrums* said that Barrie was 'a man who could make copy out of the bones of his grandmother'. In *When a Man's Single,* Barrie himself wrote: 'My God I would write an article, I think, on my mother's coffin'.

The psychoanalyst Sigmund Freud (born four years before Barrie) thought that great art was born of neurosis, not psychic 'normality'. It could be compared to the irritant grit in the oyster's shell which produces the pearl. Certainly, in Barrie's case, there was enough irritant grit to produce a string of sad stories.

Barrie was the third son in the family. The second son, David, was—'tall, athletic, handsome and charming, the golden boy of his mother's eye'. At the age of 13, he was killed in a skating accident. The mother, Margaret Ogilvy, went to pieces, and the 6-year-old James tried everything to compensate for the loss, copying his late brother's mannerisms and even wearing his clothes. Margaret withdrew from the world, but she encouraged James in his reading and told him stories of her young days.

Alexander, the eldest son, had done very well, was teaching in Glasgow Academy and was then appointed to be Her Majesty's Inspector of Schools, based in Dumfries. He was joined by his sister, who taught in Dumfries Academy, and young James, who spent the happiest five years of his life there, or so he said when he returned to the school as a distinguished former pupil.

Peter Pan never grew up, and neither did Barrie. He was just over five feet and one wonders how this shilpit little fellow fared in the rough and tumble of Edinburgh University around 1880. While at university, he wrote drama reviews for the Edinburgh papers and after graduation, began a journalistic career in Nottingham, back in 'our little red town' and in London.

In 1884, the *St James's Gazette* published an article based on one of his mother's tales of her childhood, *The Auld Licht Community*. His next article was rejected, but with the note—'I liked that Scotch thing; any more of those?'

There followed *An Auld Licht Funeral, An Auld Licht Courtship, An Auld Licht Scandal* and *An Auld Licht Wedding*. It was time for Barrie to set off for London on the overnight train. On his arrival at St Pancras, he saw a placard advertising 'the most warming sight in literature'—*The Rooks begin to Build*. After a minute or so in London, he had made two guineas! *Auld Licht Idylls* appeared in 1888. It was:

Not only the best book dealing exclusively with Scotch humble life, but the only book of the kind, deserving to be classed as literature, that has been published for at least a quarter of a century.

It was followed by *A Window in Thrums, The Little Minister* and *Margaret Ogilvy,* a tribute to his mother. 'Q' (Arthur Quiller-Couch, knighted in 1910, author, poet, Cambridge professor and responsible for The *Oxford Book of English Verse 1260-1900*) reviewed *A Window in Thrums*, thus:

What is the tale about? A little cottage, not specially picturesque; an invalid mother; the commonplace death of her first-born son, and the commonplace ruin of her second-born. No character is extraordinary, of plot there is nothing at all; the catastrophe might befall any young man, whatever his nationality or station of life…But search about in English literature, and where will you find a story of like quality of pathos written by an Anglo-Saxon?

A Window in Thrums in particular established Barrie at the head of 'the Kailyard school of Scottish fiction', typified by the small country town with hardworking, honest stereotypes, where virtue is rewarded and all turns out for the best in the end. The term comes from Lady Nairne, author of Jacobite and pawky poems, including:

There grows a bonny brier-bush in our kail-yard,
And white are the blossoms o't in our kail-yard.

Before re-reading *Margaret Ogilvie, by her Son* (1896), I was contemplating toe-curling sentimentality and unctuous ancestor worship, but it turned out not to be quite like that. By now, I had had some experience of aged relatives and found that Barrie may have had sentiment but not sentimentality. He portrays very well—and often with wry amusement—the dynamic between an aged parent and the offspring, a dynamic one can view every day in our nursing and care homes.

The frontispiece of Margaret Ogilvy having tea, wearing her beloved mutch, differs only from today in the wearer's fashionable attire!

The Kailyard novel is couthy, comforting and distinctively Scottish, but not so Scottish as to be inaccessible to readers in England and America. A feature of the Kailyard novel is the branch line which the hero's family uses to go down to the main line to see the hero off on the London train with tearful farewells, or to welcome him on his successful return.

(The Kirriemuir branch from the main Perth to Aberdeen Caledonian Railway, used by Barrie, was opened in 1861). The Kailyard writers were fine writers and their legacy lives on, although denigrated by the intelligentsia, with such as Garrison Keillor of Lake Wobegon, Minnesota.

But Barrie was not a couthy and comforting soul, as he went on to demonstrate with *Sentimental Tommy* (1896) and *Tommy and Grizel* (1900). As well as 'his warm, trusting, but painfully sensitive heart', Barrie showed that he could be 'as hard as nails, as cruel as the grave, as cynical as the Fiend.' At the same time, the Kailyard began to be attacked by such as George Douglas Brown in *The House with the Green Shutters* and (later) by Lewis Grassic Gibbon. In *Sunset Song,* he has the new minister describing Kinraddie as the Scots countryside itself; fathered between a kailyard and a bonnie brier bush in the lee of a house with green shutters.

Hugh MacDiarmid was particularly savage in attacking the complacency and political impassivity of the Kailyard, and for at least one generation, it was linked with tartan shortbread tins and the White Heather Club as a symbol of Scottish decadence. Now, however, the pendulum has swung back a little and some of the Kailyard writers have regained a measure of respect with a public sated with a diet of drugs, poverty and violence.

Barrie moved easily into London literary society, and from being a successful novelist to writing a disturbing play a year. (With Conan Doyle he also wrote the libretto of an opera for D'Oyly Carte, looking for a successor to Gilbert and Sullivan. It was a flop). At the same time as Ibsen was making an impact with such plays as *Hedda Gabler,* Barrie demonstrated a gift for writing plays that worked, that illuminated social issues, particularly what was known then as the 'sexual problem'—the double standard—where he was on the side of women without infringing the limits of polite society.

Although, George Bernard Shaw, his neighbour, friend and rival, thought that Barrie's plays had confirmed 'the final relegation of the 19th Century London theatre to the dust-bin', *The Admirable Crichton, Mary Rose, Dear Brutus, What Every Woman Knows* and *The Old Lady Shows Her Medals* have not disappeared completely from the theatrical world and the classical actor's repertoire.

Barrie, the man, had two sides. He could sit in a corner and be dour, silently watching all that was going on. But he could also be bright, clever and entertaining, especially with children. He had a weakness for young actresses and one of these, the 'bewitchingly flirtatious' Mary Ansell, fell in love with him. They were married in 1894.

The honeymoon was a nightmare and their life together unsatisfactory. There were no children and Barrie found a family life with other people's children. In 1908, Mary became infatuated with Gilbert Cannan, a protégé of her husband. Barrie divorced her for infidelity and she married Cannan in 1910.

Cannan turned out to be rather a mixed blessing. In 1914, he was ranked as a 'significant up-and-coming author' along with D. H. Lawrence, Compton Mackenzie and Hugh Walpole. He and Mary had no children but it was said that he had seduced Mary's maid and made her pregnant. There were affairs and in 1918, he was divorced. Cannan suffered a mental breakdown and in 1923, became a mental patient at the Priory Hospital, Roehampton—still a refuge for notabilities. He died of cancer in 1955.

Mary was left in straitened circumstances until Barrie offered to meet her once a year and made her an allowance. Barrie never discussed these matters –

but they were all good material for his output, however embarrassing for his family. Barrie never blamed Mary, or even Cannan. He knew where the fault lay and would stifle criticism by stating 'She was *perfection*'.

Barrie loved cricket but was too small to be any good at it, 'or any other sport really'. So he did what a rich and well-placed enthusiast can do, and formed his own band of strolling players, the Allahhakbarries, mistakenly thinking that *Allah akbar* meant 'Heaven help us'. His team sheets are a Roll of Honour of the literary world of the early 20th century.

Dwarfing Barrie was the imposing figure of Conan Doyle, who was good at all manly sports and had once bowled out the great W. G. Grace. In fact, the creator of Sherlock Holmes did not often get a game as he was so good, he would put off the others.

Question: What do the following authors have in common? Rudyard Kipling, G. K. Chesterton, H. G. Wells, P. G. Wodehouse, Jerome K. Jerome (*Three Men in a Boat*), A. A. Milne (*Winnie-the-Pooh*), E. W. Hornung (brother-in-law of Conan Doyle and creator of Raffles, the gentleman cricketer/burglar), Anthony Hope Hawkins (*The Prisoner of Zenda*), A. E. W. Mason (*The Four Feathers*, made into 6 films from 1915 to 2002), plus many others quite obscure to us in the 21st century.

Answer: They all played, without distinction, for the Allahhakbarries, had great fun and were written up in mock-heroic style by Barrie, who could use a whole page to describe an innings of a single run! The anecdotes abound, but one story is very illuminating. At 5 feet 2 inches, 'Tich' Freeman of Kent was the smallest player to play in Test matches for England.

He was also, despite his lack of inches, the second most prolific wicket-taker of all time in first-class cricket, taking 3776 wickets in a career from 1914 to 1936. Freeman was the only bowler ever to have taken over 300 wickets in a season (304 in 1928); a truly remarkable feat for two reasons. By the rules of the game, no bowler can bowl more than half the overs sent down in a match. And, in 1928, how many first-class games did Kent play?

So, theoretically, how many potential victims were available to Freeman in a season? And how many opportunities were 'lost' because of bad weather or because the opposition, for a variety of reasons, did not all bat in both innings of a match?

So Barrie, characteristically silent, was watching Freeman bowling for Kent one day. He turned to his neighbour and asked him: 'Would you say Freeman was a fast bowler?'

'Oh no,' his neighbour replied. 'Freeman is a slow bowler. He relies on guile and spin.'

'Well, I think he is very fast,' said Barrie.

An interesting photograph of 1922, taken at the opening of new sports fields at Dundee University College, shows Barrie bowling left-handed to Field Marshal Douglas Haig. He (Barrie) is wearing a trilby hat, a generous muffler and a thick jacket. His stance is so open and his arm so low that he cannot have presented much difficulty to the batsman, who could certainly still hit a golf ball well at 61!

But left-handedness may account for some of Barrie's difficulties. As a left-hander, he would certainly have been forced, perhaps brutally, to write with the right hand, as all Scots boys and girls were until well into the 20th century. However, in 1929, Barrie's right hand developed a kind of writer's cramp and he switched back to using his left. His writing became legible for the first time since childhood, suggesting that it was easier for him.

Kathleen Bruce, a sculptress in her own right, was courted by Gilbert Cannan and Captain Robert Falcon Scott. After a year, she accepted the latter and spurned the former, who turned to Mary Barrie for consolation. Barrie, who was the godfather of the Scotts' son, Peter, who was to become a famous naturalist, partly financed Scott's expedition to the South Pole. Scott's party trained for their assault on the South Pole in Glen Prosen, 10Km north of Kirriemuir.

One of the last letters that Scott wrote, as he lay near to death 'in a very comfortless spot', was to Barrie. In it, he seems to be apologising for some misunderstanding we do not know about and 'more practically' asks Barrie to help my widow and my boy…your godson…I leave my poor girl and your godson…Do what you can to get their claims recognised.

Lady Scott (as she now was), perhaps wisely, declined Barrie's offer to be Peter's guardian but Barrie continued to support the boy, who visited him weekly for several years.

In 2002 and 2009, suggestions were made that Barrie was a paedophile. He certainly loved children, was good with them and probably enjoyed their company better than that of adults. Best known is his relationship with the Llewelyn Davies boys and their parents. It began in Kensington Gardens where

Barrie met the boys with their nannies and entertained them with jokes and stories and by waggling his ears.

As 'Uncle Jim' he became part of their family life. There were stories and adventures around the Round Pond in Kensington and Black Lake Cottage in Surrey. Being Barrie, all this fun and drama became the raw material for *Peter Pan* and other works.

As well as being enthralling company, he was rich and powerful and was able to give the boys opportunities their parents could not provide. Sylvia (Llewelyn Davies) was beautiful and from a theatrical background. She was well aware of the dangers of the situation, but her 'innate and underlying tendency towards melancholy' was more than 'counterbalanced by an appetite for luxury'.

Arthur (Llewelyn Davies) was a struggling lawyer. The kindest of parents, he knew that Barrie presented no threat to the marriage, but must still have felt some resentment that this 'intrusive little Scotsman' could provide for his children what he could not.

Peter Pan is not all sickly sentimentality. Barrie has his vicious side. The lovely little lambs that gambol about in springtime grow into clumsy, smelly sheep. In 1907, Arthur died of cancer, aged 44. Three years later, Sylvia died, also of cancer and aged 44. The boys' nurse, Mary Hodgson, continued to care for them, Barrie continued to provide housing, education and financial support and three of the Du Mauriers (Sylvia's family) were guardians.

Of the closest boys, George was killed in Flanders in 1915. Michael died, aged 21, in strange circumstances in 1921. He was the only one of the boys who could not swim, yet he drowned with an inseparable companion near a monument to two other Oxford men who were drowned in 1843. Jack (1894-1959) was the least loyal to Barrie, at times suspicious of the interloper 'saving us all from ruin'. A career in the Navy and marriage took him out of the closest contact with 'the dearest fellow in the world'.

Peter had a hard time at Eton, where he was mercilessly ragged as 'the real Peter Pan', a description that was to haunt him all his life. At 19, he walked into a commission in the 60th (King's Royal Rifles) Foot. After two months, he was invalided home, with eczema and shell-shock. Although, he was awarded the Military Cross in 1918, his service was such an ordeal that he could not write to 'Uncle Jim' about it and in later life, avoided all reference to it.

Shy and retiring, in 1926, Peter found his own much-respected publishing house. And in 1960, Peter walked into the local underground station and threw himself beneath an oncoming train.

The press had a field day:

Barrie's Peter Pan killed by a London subway train.

The Boy who never grew up is dead.

Peter Pan stood alone to die

Peter Pan's Death Leap

Peter Pan commits suicide.

The Tragedy of Peter Pan.

Nico, the youngest boy, was lovable and charming and because he was the last to die (in 1980), he was the most accessible to modern journalists. We live in a climate in which behaviour like Barrie's might be regarded with great suspicion, or in which the great ones might be allowed to enjoy themselves inappropriately without censure, or be accused by rogues or fantasists. Nico was clearly not disinterested, nor was he under oath, when he remarked:

I don't believe that Uncle Jim ever experienced what one might call a stirring in the undergrowth for anyone—man, woman, adult or child. He was an innocent, which is why he could write Peter Pan.

I have a gut feeling that he was right.

Thrums played an important part in Barrie's life. He did not, as some others might have done, abandon his place of birth as he moved on. The trail will prove that.

Sandra Affleck, in *The Little Red Town and JMB,* suggests that while Barrie was sauntering around the shops during his 1899 visit, he noticed:
David Young's High Street shop selling 'Thrums Rock', Duncan's grocery selling 'Thrums Whisky', AP Mill in the Roods selling both 'Thrums' and 'Little Minister' cigarettes, and Burnett's selling their 'Thrums Make' of boots? He couldn't have failed to see J Dow & Sons 'Thrums Grocery Store', and may even have bought a copy of James Stirton's book, 'Thrums and Its Glens'.

But for anyone to find their way to Thrums is difficult. They will not find it on an Ordnance Survey map or on an old Caledonian Railway timetable. Thrums does not, nor did it ever, exist. Thrums was a creation of Barrie's mind. Kirriemuir was the template for his imagination, but imagine the reactions of the good folk of Kirrie if they had been identified in Barrie's stories. Being placed in Thrums was bad enough.

Why Thrums? Why not Drummlydubs or Tannochbrae? It fits exactly. In weaving, thrums are the ends of the warp threads or scraps of waste thread. But also a thrum is 'a perverse streak in a person's character, a whim, fit of ill-humour', which fits exactly the Kirrie Auld Licht character, and Barrie's own character, his humour of understatement, his wry innuendo, his irony or veiled mockery.

Incidentally, Kirriemuir itself is not without some qualification as a 'weel-kent' place. Indeed, it may even be better-known internationally than Thrums. The North-east of Scotland is remarkable for the survival of folk culture and the Doric, its special 'speak'. About the time that Barrie was dominating the West End theatre, Gavin Greig (a schoolmaster) and the Reverend James Duncan began collecting the folk songs of the north-east, 1933 of them, unexpurgated. Many were bothy ballads, sung and circulated by single farm workers lodged on the farm and confined to a bothy after work.

The 1930s was the heyday of the Americanisation of popular culture in Britain, of jazz, swing and Hollywood. John Reith, son of a United Free Church minister, the first Director-General of the BBC, and later to be 1st Baron Reith of Stonehaven, did something to try to stem the tide.

John Strachan (1875-1958) was a farmer and tradition bearer near Turriff in Aberdeenshire, who took his folk songs into schools and WRI concerts, with his concertina on his knee. He was not the stereotypical folk singer from the berryfields of Blairgowrie, born in a traveller's hovel and living an irregular life to an early death. His family had several farms. He went to Robert Gordon's College, could write excellent Robert Gordon's prose and, in his turn, acquired several farms.

But he was firmly rooted in the land and its past. As a folk singer in 1930, he was already so well known that an American from Harvard came over to record him. In 1935, a radio programme (The Farm Year) was broadcast live from his farm. One John Mearns sang *The Bonnie Lass o' Fyvie* on the programme and went on to keep cornkisters and Scottish country dancing regularly on the air till the 1950s.

A measure of Strachan can be obtained from two paragraphs of the broadcast he made from Crichie on the Christmas Day radio programme, following on from King George V's speech to the empire.

Ay, ay, London, I hear ye. A happy Christmas to you an' a'. Noo, fat was I tell't tae speak tae ye aboot? Oh, ay, I ws to tell ye faur I bide. Weel, I bide in a fairm in the north-east o' Scotland—an' I'm sitti' in' the kitchie o' that fairm I' noo, an' lookin' oot o' the window. Mebbe you wadna ca' the view awfu' bonnie, I ken it looks bare kin',an' I ken it has nae trees worth speakin' aboot, but I wadna leave't, nae ye gied me a thoosan' acres o' the promised laan'.

And to conclude:

Weel, I some think I've near aboot said a' 'at I can, except that the wife an' me, ay, an' the hail o' Scotland, wish ye a Gweed Christmas and a Gweed New Year—ay, fan it comes—like. We send special greetings tae a' fairmers and countryfolk, mair especially tae the fairmer, far ayont the sea, that's tae speak next in this programme. His name's Mr Smithers, and his fairm, I'm tellt, is about ten mile from Cape Toon in South Africa. Ay, ay, Mr Smithers, can you hear me? The wife and me send oor best respects tae you and your family in South Africa.

Hamish Henderson says of Strachan and *The Ball of Kirriemuir*:

Strachan must have known many bawdy songs but seemed reluctant to sing them. He gave us a fragment of *The Ball of Kirriemuir*…At the end, he says 'It's a terrible een.' (one).

Why was it terrible? Because of its length? Or because of its unsuitability for mixed company? In the Strachan recording I remember, which is not too colourful, he finishes:

Here's tae auld Kirriemear
And here's tae the Ball
I canna sing anither note
My thrapple's ower small.

The Ball o' Kirriemuir may have been 'written' in the 1880s, and may relate to an actual annual fixture in the social calendar of the Angus town. Or it may be pure (?) fantasy or the wishful thinking of single men cooped up without female company. Basically, it starts 'Fower-and-twenty virgins cam doon frae Inverness…' and goes on and on for many verses, describing every possible eventuality known to man, and woman!

The tune is quite catchy, in strathspey rhythm, and, as *Bonny Jean*, was first published in the mid-18th century.

It is number 4828 in the Roud Folk Song Index, and is a real folk song in the sense that it is popular and earthy, and is being added to and rewritten all the time. It entered the repertoire of rugby clubs and student bodies, being well-suited to the convivial evening where each participant has to sing or make up another verse, dirtier than the previous one.

Surfing the net, one finds that it has been recorded, renamed and copied all over the world. The original is dirty but witty, but an American version is just dirty and crass. People like Vishakhadatta Diwakar and Krishna Sethuraman want the words supplied while an American wants to go back to Aberdeen University where he first heard the song.

Barrie was prolific, yet his fame has narrowed down to one living work—yet the name of Kirriemuir has spread round the world, despite its politically incorrect association.

Another Kirriemuir association may now be out-of-date. After Barrie's time, some people would have referred to 'the Kirriemuir career'.

Before the World War 1, farm workers and the like must have been jealous of the country schoolmaster, who had an easy job, long holidays and a regular salary. Walter Wingate expressed this very well in *The Dominie's Happy Lot*, which concludes:

Oh! Leezie, Leezie. Fine and easy

Is a job like yon-

Sax weeks to jaunt and gallivant,

And aye the pay gaun on!

JC Milne in *Dominie Dandy (Two)* describes the virtues of 'the couthy country skweel', or schoolmaster.

Fae Monday till Friday nicht I'd yark the learnin in

Though I widna touch the fancy frills, for that wid be a sin!

Nae drawin, singin. dancin – they're the cantrips o' the Deil!

Na, I widna hae sic ongauns in my couthy country skweel.

Bot O the reams o' writin a' my littlins aye wid dae!

And siccan lists o' spellin's ilka nicht they'd learn for me!

And dyod the aul' Director wid dance a highland reel

Gin he cam', but that's nae likely, to my couthy country skweel.

So, there we have the raw material for the Kirriemuir career. Find yourself a nice country school, or a nice small-town school like Webster's Seminary in Kirriemuir, founded in 1835 with John Webster's bequest. Settle in, do all the right things, play golf in summer, church on Sundays, the basics during the week, mollify the parents, no frills, keep your nose clean. Then, after a suitable interval, you are ready to move on, perhaps like Barrie's brother, to be an Inspector of Schools.

The Trail

The visitor to Kirriemuir is most likely to approach it from the south, from Glamis across the flat plain of Strathmore to what are in effect the foothills of the Grampians. Entering the lower part of Kirriemuir, the visitor will be struck by the two abandoned jute mills, abandoned but not derelict, shoehorned into the rolling slopes by the river.

1. All the older part of the town is built of the local Old Red Sandstone. Durable yet workable, its red-brown surfaces glow in the low sun of winter. The result is a collection of fine, sturdy, handsome buildings reflecting the town's prosperity a century ago, although the narrow twisting streets and steep slopes make their appreciation difficult.

The Square is, however, more open and there is room for a pedestrian area with a plinth and a small statue of Peter Pan. (This is its second site, as it was vandalised on its original site.)

Follow the High Street up the hill, turn right along St Malcolm's Wynd into Reform Street—a reminder of the political activities of the nineteenth century weavers.

2. At the start of the Brechin Road is a small **Barrie Garden,** with an Art Nouveau Barrie Fountain. It has a suitable inscription and four panels inspired by Peter Pan.
3. A few yards further along the road is **Barrie's Birthplace**, owned and managed by the National Trust for Scotland. Known as 'The Tenements', it is actually two houses and is quite conspicuous, having been harled and whitewashed, totally out of keeping with the rest of Kirriemuir.

The houses are built right up to the road, so that access is round the back where doors and windows face south. In the yard is a little wash-house with a chimney. A keek through the window reveals the copper in which the washing was boiled.

(In the 1940s, my family spent a lot of time with my grandfather in Inverurie, not a million miles from Thrums. There was a shared wash-house for four houses, and the only bath my young brother and sister had was in the copper at the end of the day when the clothes were hung out and the water had cooled.)

Barrie's birthplace is numbers 9 and 11, but the Barrie house was only number 9. The entrance is through number 11 whose downstairs room is the reception and sales area.

The way through the house is enlivened by a narrative on the walls, illustrated with text, quotations and photographs. We pass into what was the downstairs room of the Barrie house. It has a flagstone floor, a kitchen range, a grandfather clock by I Bower of 'Kerrymuir', and modern cases displaying Barrie's books. Incongruously, the room is dominated by Barrie's desk from Adelphi Terrace in London.

At one stage, this room would have housed Barrie Senior's loom and his store of yarn. It then became the parlour and six hair-bottomed chairs were bought for it on the day Barrie was born, 6 May 1860. (Margaret had saved up a pound note and 30 threepenny bits, approximately £1.40, for six good chairs!)

Upstairs, the corresponding room would have been the kitchen and has another fireplace and kitchen tools. There are rag rugs on the floor and a 'wag at the wa' clock in the corner. A 'skeiner' or skein winder has thrums hanging over it (PLATE 6a).

The bedroom next door has a nice cast iron fireplace, a box bed, Margaret Ogilvie's nursing chair and a cradle (not Barrie's). Also in this room are two of the famous parlour chairs. Barrie was the ninth of ten children. Where did they all fit in?

Over to the 'Trophy Room', which is the upstairs of number 11. On the landing, two interesting documents are displayed, a multi-layered 'Family of Barrie' and J. M. B's birth certificate, on which David Barrie is described as a 'Linen Manufacturer'—a slight exaggeration.

The Trophy Room is devoted to Barrie's fame. There is his portrait by Lavery, the most popular in his time. There are playbills and photographs of those who appeared in his plays. A photo shows him receiving the Freedom of Kirriemuir and a certificate grants him the Freedom of the City of London. There is his draft of his Rectorial Address on 'Courage' which he gave at St Andrews in 1922.

This was a great day, especially for such a modest little man. When he arrived at the station, the boisterous male students unhitched the horses from his carriage and pulled it themselves. It was 'like being a royalist in a tumbril en route to the guillotine'.

His student audience was held for an hour as he told them they needed the courage to challenge the views of their elders, otherwise they might be led once again into a world war. As he so poignantly put it:

Look around and see how much share youth has now the war is over. You got a handsome share while it lasted.

If you prefer to leave things as they, are we will probably fail you again.

They were to beware of people who mindlessly supported military action. After all, he said, 'Hell hath no fury like a non-combatant'.

His final touch was to bring out and read the letter that Captain Scott had written to him while dying in his tent in the Antarctic.

On the lighter side, especially interesting is the material surviving from the opening of the cricket pavilion on 7 June 1930. As we know, Barrie was a cricketer of very modest ability, but he clearly had a talent for drawing others together and having fun. Two Australians added to the jollity of that day.

In a glass case is a bat used by C. G. Macartncy, the 'Governor General', who had played his last Test in 1926. An excellent player (2131 runs and 45 wickets in 35 Tests) he was:

One of the most brilliant and attractive right-handed batsmen in the history of Australian cricket. Daring and confident, he possessed a quickness of eye, hand and foot, a perfection of timing which made him a menace to the best of bowlers.

In 1921:

He constantly did things that would be quite wrong for an ordinary batsman, but by success justified all his audacities.

Arthur Mailey was a leg-break bowler who also played his last Test in 1926, in 21 Tests having amassed the frustrating total of 99 wickets. He had some brilliant games. His 9 wickets for 121 at Melbourne in 1920-21 remains the best Australian bowling feat in Test matches. All too often, however, his fate was to plug away cheerfully on the shirtfront Australian wickets of the period.

Three times he was hit for over 300 runs in a match. (No other bowler has achieved this remarkable feat more than once). When Victoria scored the record first-class total of 1107 in 1926-27, Mailey bowled 64 eight-ball overs, went for 362 runs—yet contrived to take four wickets. He was no great shakes as a batsman, but at Sydney in 1924-25, he helped to set up the Australian record for the 10th wicket—a record which stood until 2013.

In 1930, both of these great players were in England as journalists covering the Australian touring team. What does it tell us about Barrie that these great cricketers—great in character as well as in achievement—should come north to a little Scottish town to play in a light-hearted game with a hopeless enthusiast?

4. Emerge from the birthplace and turn right along the Brechin Road. On the left, note the gateposts and drive of **The Manse**. A Barrie Society plaque tells us that this was the entrance to The Auld Licht Manse while a 'Private Property' sign deters intrusion. Going up the neighbouring drive shows that the manse site has been transformed into a little modern enclave.

5. Continue along the Brechin Road, past the modern Barrie Place, to **Cemetery Road**. Climb to the cemetery gates, turn left and follow the signposts—first on the level, then up a steep winding road—to Barrie's Grave. This is one of the most beautiful and beautifully kept cemeteries in the country, and the Barrie family plot is nicely placed on the brow of the hill. There are three gravestones, with Barrie's name discreetly tucked in with the names of fourteen other family members.

However, he has his own little plaque at a slightly lower level, simply inscribed 'J M Barrie, Playwright' on an Art Nouveau stage, with open curtains and an enthusiastic audience in silhouette in the stalls (PLATE 6b).

6. Follow the cemetery road round to the top of the hill and go through a metal gate on the left. The gate, or its predecessor, was the wicket for the young Barrie, so it was very appropriate, if ironical, that this self-proclaimed Scotsman on the make who fell completely in love with the most English of games, should remember those days.

Ahead is the **cricket pavilion** which Barrie gifted to the town when he received the Freedom in 1930. Around are the public park and a children's Peter Pan Adventure Park. Where the cricket is played must be one of the least prepossessing pitches outside Afghanistan. A great deal of fuss is made about the slope at Lords', but at Kirriemuir the slope is formidable and must make things very difficult for both batsman and bowler.

At the official opening, the Allahhakbarries comprehensively beat West of Scotland—we are spared details of how this unlikely result was achieved.

A few minutes directly downhill takes us back to The Square, where we started.

Chapter Eight

Brotherly Confusion
Colonel James Macleod and Calgary

Calgary is the largest city in Alberta and the fifth biggest in Canada. Before the Europeans came, the area that was to become Calgary was inhabited by the Blackfoot, Blood, Peigan and Tsuu Tina First Nations peoples, all part of the Blackfoot Confederacy. David Thompson (sounds like a Scot) was the first recorded European to visit the area.

He was a Hudson's Bay Company trader and cartographer, who spent the winter of 1787 with a band of Peigan encamped along the Bow River. John Glenn (another Scot?) was the first documented European settler in the Calgary area, in 1873.

The site became a post of the North West Mounted Police (now the Royal Canadian Mounted Police), with the responsibilities of protecting the western plains from US whisky traders, and protecting the fur trade. The 1875 fort was originally named Fort Brisebois, after NWMP Ephrem-A Brisebois.

James Macleod (1836-1894) was born in Drynoch, Skye, from which his family emigrated to Ontario in 1845. Macleod took all the opportunities available in the New World and rose to become colonel and the second Commissioner of the North-West Mounted Police. He was a militia officer, lawyer, magistrate, judge and politician in Alberta.

During and after the American Civil War, Canada was much troubled by malcontents coming over the border with the United States. In 1866, there were 350,000 Fenians who had sworn an oath 'to free and regenerate Ireland from the yoke of England'. A British schooner was captured off Long Island and 'Colonel' John O'Neil invaded Ontario, withdrawing over the US border.

In 1870, he tried again, returned again in haste, was imprisoned in the US, was released and instigated another rebellion, this time in Manitoba, but was arrested before he crossed the border.

In 1869, the Hudson Bay Territory was transferred to the Dominion of Canada and incorporated into Manitoba. Not all were happy with this and Louis Riel styled himself a general, seized the company's treasury, seized Fort Garry (Winnipeg), imprisoned, murdered and maltreated British subjects. The Canadian militia and a force of British regulars, who came 1,118 miles under the command of Colonel Garnet Wolseley, stifled the rebellion. Riel escaped before the British arrived.

(Sir Garnet Wolseley had a distinguished career in Burma, the Crimea, the Indian Mutiny, West Africa and Egypt, ending up as field marshal, viscount and commander-in-chief of the Forces. Around 1900, the phrase 'everything's all Sir Garnet' meant 'all is well'. At the other end of the promotion ladder, Private Timothy O'Hea won the Victoria Cross for putting out a fire in an ammunition wagon, perhaps the only occasion in which the VC was won for bravery when not in the presence of the enemy.)

Riel was back again in 1885, feeding on the resentment felt at the opening up of the North-West Territory. This time, no British troops were engaged. The Canadian Militia Force was headed up by a general and there was a battle at Batoche, in which only 850 men took part. The rebels were defeated, Riel captured, tried and hanged. Thus ended the more serious of the Fenian and other rebellious troubles.

Alberta was too far west to be affected by these excitements—the railway only reached Calgary two years before Riel's Rebellion. But, as a major in the militia, Macleod saw military service in the Fenian Raids. In Alberta, he put an end to the illegal whisky trade (although, he was reputed to have had 'an enormous capacity for "whiskey", which he could consume in large quantities, apparently with no effort'), and established good relations with the First Nation peoples (as the Canadians call the native Americans).

With his connections, he could have made a fortune, but was too honest—on his death he was reputed to have left behind 'a wife, five children and 8 dollars'.

In the 1870s, he took a holiday in Scotland and was a summer guest at Calgary Castle, on the island of Mull. Why there? We do not know, but I suspect it was not coincidental; he may have been searching for island roots, certainly on Skye and perhaps also on Mull.

On Macleod's return to Canada in 1876, he suggested that Fort Brisebois be renamed Fort Calgary—just as it was about to become a boom town. The Canadian Pacific Railway reached the area in 1883. A year later, it was officially incorporated as a town in 1884. With the railway and 'free land', the entire area grew rapidly and steadily.

Calgary became the centre for a thriving agricultural region, with associated food processing. (The Calgary Stampede, started in 1912, is said to be 'the greatest outdoor show on earth').

In 1894, Calgary became a City. By 2011, it had over a million inhabitants, making it the largest city in Alberta, and the fifth largest in Canada. Oil and gas in the Prairies was another multiplier. Calgary: 'is home to the second-most corporate head offices in Canada among the country's 800 largest corporations'

And the headquarters of the Canadian Pacific Railway was moved from Montreal to Calgary in 1996. In 1988, Calgary became the first Canadian city to host the Olympic Winter Games.

The link between Calgary, Alberta and Calgary, Mull is clearly a very tenuous one, entirely dependent on Colonel James Macleod's holiday, which, as we have seen, was probably combined with a search for island roots, certainly on Skye and perhaps also on Mull.

There were several MacLeods around Calgary, and if this were a work of fiction, one could say that Colonel James Macleod was the grandson of one of the crofters evicted from Mull, settling in Skye. 1845 was the first year of the great Potato Famine, which hit the Highlands and Islands almost as much as it did Ireland, and the MacLeods might have been forced into emigration at that time. But more work needs to be done on this troubled time!

Calgary Bay in Mull is seventh on the list of Britain's Secret Beaches. This is not surprising, as at the head of the bay is a long curving strand (Traigh Chalgaraidh) of brilliant white sand, pollution free and backed by a spread of *machair,* the short springy turf of the Hebrides.

Looking out to sea there are steep slopes and cliffs on each side, mostly the terraced lava flows so typical of Mull. As for being secret, Calgary is on the north-west corner of Mull, only attainable after a long journey on the mainland to Oban, then a ferry to Craignure on the east coast of the island, followed by a switchback on single-track roads.

Calgary itself is a scattering of houses, ancient and modern. Calgary Farm has grass fields, cattle and sheep, but has also acquired a café and an art gallery. An old boat, painted white and inscribed 'Calgary Art in Nature', sits in a field.

The car park with the usual picnic benches is on the machair, which is a Conservation Area. An upturned boat serves as an information centre and behind it, a little kiosk sells Isle of Mull Ice Cream. A notice informs us about the Mull Otter Group. (Mull has one of the highest incidences of otters in Britain. It has 10-12 otter deaths on the roads every year).

The connection between the two Calgaries is obvious. We all know about the Highland Clearances, the failure of the potato crop in 1846, the consequent famine and the possible sixty thousand who left the western Highlands for the United States, Canada and Australia.

The obvious explanation for the two Calgaries is that a shipload of Mull folk was transported to Canada and were settled in a place which they named Calgary, from their place of origin. A common enough pattern, but just not true in this case.

According to the Royal Commission on the Ancient and Historical Monuments of Scotland, now incorporated into Historic Environment Scotland:

Pont's map of the late 16th century records the existence of a farm or township at 'Inue'; the lands of 'Imvie' are referred to about 1670, and the name is given as 'Inive' in 1739. By the last quarter of the 18th century, the township seems to have become absorbed within the neighbouring farm of Frachadil, and it is not mentioned by name in the census of the Argyll estates made in 1779, or on Langlands's map of 1801.

However, in the window of the Mull Museum in Tobermory, there is an enlarged photocopy of Langlands's map, on which 'Inive' is clearly marked.

The twenty or so families of Inivie, like many on Mull, must have had a hard time of it. The walls of their modest dwellings still stand (PLATE 7a). Around them, on their steep hillside, are round kailyards of stone (to keep out the free-ranging livestock) and kilns for drying the barley and oats grown in this high rainfall area.

Where the land flattens out a little, above the township, were cultivation rigs, for corn and potatoes, which had become the staple diet. Seaweed, for fertiliser, from the rocky shore below may have been carried up in creels. A track from the old pier up to the township may have been used for pack ponies, if the crofters had them.

Seaweed might have been an important element in the local economy. During the Napoleonic wars, kelp was harvested from the seashore and burnt to yield barilla—sodium carbonate for soap manufacture. This was dirty and exhausting work, but it was paid. For the lairds, it was a bonanza until 1815 when cheap Spanish barilla finished off our kelp industry. The results were catastrophic.

Hugh McLean, the Laird of Coll (8 miles as the sea eagle flies from Calgary), tried to remedy the situation by expatriating his population to Australia, suggesting that each family be given 100 acres by the Colonial Office while he should be given a further 20,000 acres, paid for by the Treasury.

McLean wrote:

Sir, Believing that the Australian Colonies are more immediately under your direction and feeling assured of the personal interest you will take in the subject, I beg leave to communicate the substance of my letter to Lord Glenelg offering to settle in Australia, clear of Convict Contamination, 3000 of my poor countrymen without expense to government. I am a Highland Proprietor who having lost one third of his income by the annihilation of kelp manufacture have consequently a large surplus population which must either ruin me, starve, or emigrate.

These poor people naturally look to me for the help I am utterly unable to afford, and I feel most keenly the responsibility of recommending their going into the almost certain destruction of Convict contact and example. They are themselves aware of their great danger and importune me for location apart. This I endeavour to obtain for them by my offer.

Glenelg is a popular tourist destination and beach-side suburb of Adelaide, South Australia. Named after Lord Glenelg, a British Cabinet Minister and Secretary of State for War and the Colonies, it was established in 1836 and was the oldest European settlement on mainland South Australia. Another Glenelg is a huge parish on the mainland of Scotland, opposite Skye, and, as the crow flies, about 45 miles from Coll and Calgary.

It had the same problems as Mull and the rest of the west coast of Scotland. So Lord Glenelg would have been quite conversant with the background to McLean's suggestion.

Not surprisingly, McLean's offer was declined, but a great number of Scots did subsequently emigrate to Australia, the United States and Canada.

In 1811, the Earl of Selkirk set up the Red River Colony in what is now Manitoba, as an outlet for distressed Scots. The early days were difficult, but Selkirk set a good example by settling there himself in 1817, putting the colony on its feet before his death in 1820. On the other hand, MacDonell of Glengarry led 300 of his people from Knoydart to settle in Canada, but after three years beat a retreat to his ancestral estate.

Many others drifted south to the industrialising towns and cities, or to areas like Flanders Moss where land reclamation was dependent on new settlers.

We might have arrived in Mull via the Lochaline ferry, and on the way visited Aoineadh Mor, where the Scottish proprietor, Miss Christina Stewart of Edinburgh, cleared the township with a fair degree of brutality.

Where did Inivie fit into this big picture? In 1817, the property came into the hands of Captain Allan McAskill of Mornish, the estate to the north and 'local tradition avers that the inhabitants of the township were evicted by this proprietor', no doubt as part of an improvement programme which included extending an earlier laird's house into Calgary Castle.

Who do you think you are? is a highly successful BBC TV programme in which interesting people, with expert assistance, research their past—often with disturbing results! In 2006, David Tennant, born David Macdonald, and at that time best known as the fourth Doctor Who? was a subject. His grandfather worked in the Glasgow shipyards and Tennant started by assuming that he, Tennant, was a Lowlander.

However, he and Brian Thomson, a genealogist, discovered from the 1861 census that Donald MacLeod had been born in Mull, in Kilninian parish.

Off we went, through beautiful scenery, to the 1755 parish church of Kilninian, a huge parish of 121 square miles in the north of Mull. There the baptismal records showed that Charles Macleod and Catherine MacNiven had had their son, Donald, baptised on 1 August 1819 and that he was one of ten children. They lived at Inivie. Where was that?

The two researchers could not find it on the map, but the next scene was at Calgary Bay, with Meg Douglass, the local historian, pointing out to Tennant the salient features of the landscape before leading him up the track to the ruins of Inivie.

Filmed on a sunny day in early spring, everything was crystal clear. Around one ruined black house, the pair discussed the details of the crofters' lives, including the water supply—a tiny burn for the people and their livestock. Tennant straddled it and found it good! A shot of Calgary House was shown, emphasising the social distance between landowner and tenant. This led on to the issue of the Clearances, which Tennant found disturbing. And then, it was time to turn to another grandparent and follow his tracks.

What happened to the crofters cleared from Inivie from 1817? A Gaelic poem said:

Some went across the ocean,
Some went to the graveyard,
And where are the others?
No one knows.

No one, to my knowledge, has researched Inivie but it is likely that the people merely dispersed for a short distance. No fishing villages were set up. There was no re-allocation on new plots. There were no mass emigrations from Mull as early as this. They seem just to have faded away, with succeeding generations drifting south.

Inivie was an entity from the 16th century at least, but it came to an end in the early 19th century. Long before the other Calgary took off.

The Trail

The starting point is the car park on the north side of the machair, just above the strand (Traigh Chalgaraidh) of Calgary Bay. A pleasant walk on an old road along the north shore of the loch, brings one to an old pier, now in some disrepair. This was built about 1870 to shelter the puffers bringing in coal for the Mornish estate, and for transporting sheep out to the Treshnish Islands for summer grazing.

Adjacent are the imposing gateposts of a substantial storage building whose stone walls (dykes) morph into an imposing volcanic dyke which marches uphill.

Follow the old road, now a track, uphill to the 21st century equivalent of a summer shieling—a big ramshackle shed sheltering some boats and haymaking machinery, a sheep fank with a water supply, a dipping facility and an old caravan for overnight subsistence. There are a few sheep around, reminding us of why this land was cleared. Proceed beyond this, uphill, till, just before the track seems to be petering out, you see on the skyline above an old road quarry the ruins—to wall head height—of a traditional croft house or black house.

This is a good point at which to stop—like Tennant and his guide—for breath and to imagine what it would have been like to carry a creel of wet seaweed up here for the so-called lazy beds above the township.

Turn uphill and follow the burn for a couple of hundred yards. On either side, you will see scattered about abandoned cottages, the remains of smaller buildings and mysterious stretches of wall. In October, the vegetation is at its most luxurious and only the cottages stick out. It is a good idea to go above the settlement.

Looking down, there does seem to be a rough pattern. On either side of the burn, there is a very rough line of houses, almost like steps on a staircase, while over to the left (east) on slightly flatter ground, there is a more random mixture of houses, barns and kailyards.

Fortunately, the Royal Commission on Ancient and Historical Monuments of Scotland surveyed the area meticulously in 1980 and as a result, reconstructing the settlement and imagining life there is quite easy.

The houses, although on a south-facing slope, presented an end to the gales off the Atlantic. Each was about 10 metres long, rectangular with rounded corners. Tennant commented on how low the walls were, the roofs, timber and thatch having been destroyed at the time of eviction or merely left to decay. To the untrained eye, all ruined black houses look much the same, but, although very basic, the houses at Inivie were not completely unsophisticated.

They were exceptionally well built. Most of the stone used was local and random, although some came from a nearby *dun*, or Iron Age fort. Carefully selected blocks cut from the local Tertiary basalt, set in clay mortar, were set to frame windows and doors. The external corners of the houses are rounded and are really quite elegant, some of the larger stones having been hammer-dressed to a curve.

There are three very distinct types of thatched house in the West Highlands and the Inivie houses belong to a class which occupied the territory from north Argyll (including north Mull) along the west coast as far north as Sutherland and including Skye. There is evidence to suggest that the houses were not the result of a series of individual decisions. Inivie may not have been a planned settlement but it certainly shows the effect of some overall direction.

The houses are in some rough order, are of very similar size and plan, and look as if they have been constructed by the same hands at the same time—perhaps in the 1790s under the guidance of a reforming local laird—no doubt replacing the earlier, untidy, Inivie. If this is true, the township may only have been fully active for about twenty-five years.

Fig 16:
Plan of Inivie, 1980
(Crown Copyright HES)

The barns had two doors, on opposite walls, one facing south-west, so that the prevailing wind could dry the grain. Water for twenty households and their animals must have been a problem as the stream through the township is tiny. Meg Douglass suggested that there might have been a little dam, creating a pool, from which the livestock would have had to be excluded.

RCAHMS suggest there may have been a little horizontal water mill—common in the Highlands and Islands—for grinding the grain. Otherwise, it would have had to be the hand quern.

East of the township is some flatter ground which was cultivated, and where RCAHMS say there are the remains of rigs. In October, I could not find these. Down by the shore, there is some flatter, but wet, ground. I could see no evidence of cultivation there, nor of people having lived there.

Tennant's reaction to Inivie was astonishment at the difficulty of wresting a living from such a hostile environment. Most visitors will feel the same. We do not know the details of the clearance of Inivie but we must ask ourselves whether a fresh start, however brought about, was not such a bad idea for Donald MacLeod and his fellows in 1814?

Chapter Nine

A Postman's Nightmare
Sir Patrick Geddes and Perth

Turn by turn, and even simultaneously, Patrick Geddes (1854-1932) was a botanist, economist, sociologist, producer of pageants, public lecturer, writer of verse, art critic, publisher, civic reformer, town planner, Victorian moralist, provocative agnostic and academic revolutionary. He was Sir Patrick Geddes for only fifty-two days, dying in Montpellier from an infection picked up in London at the time of the investiture.

In his time, he was internationally influential. After his death, he fell out of favour, but his ideas were rediscovered in the 1970s and he is now seen as a major figure in the environmental movement. Pheroze Barucha, an Indian former student at Geddes's *Collège des Écossais,* said:
He re-kindled the creative spark in you…He just set you on fire with love of this earth and with desire to cleanse it, to beautify it and to rebeautify it, to build and rebuild it.

Lewis Mumford described him as 'a vigorous institution', while the title of Paddy Kitchen's Geddes book was 'a most unsettling person'.

On the other hand, Alex Law, Professor of Sociology at Abertay University, described him as 'a failed sociologist'.

Although, he was born in Ballater, Patrick Geddes spent his formative years in and around Perth, on the lower slopes of Kinnoull Hill, on the east side of the Tay. Perth was a good place to grow up in. With a supportive family, a delightfully varied environment and a county town of some importance, he was able to benefit from a reasonably intellectual society.

Many of his ideas stemmed from his youthful days. In later years, he was able to return to recharge his batteries, to renew acquaintance with his roots and—it has to be said—seek financial support for his latest scheme.

Perth, as a place, was fundamental to Geddes's development and understanding. What kind of a place was Geddes's Perth? In brief, an interesting environment with an eventful history.

Perth's location is interesting. On the west bank of the mighty River Tay, deep and fast, about the upper limit of the effect of tides, with the result that it has always been, and still is, a modest port for seagoing ships. It is just about the lowest bridge point of the river—so, like Stirling, it became an important communication node and a kind of regional capital.

The land around is mainly derived from the Old Red Sandstone and is as agriculturally productive as almost any land in these latitudes. Sir Walter Scott put his cards on the table when he started *The Fair Maid of Perth* thus:

Among all the provinces in Scotland, if an intelligent stranger were asked to describe the most varied and the most beautiful, it is probable he would name the county of Perth.

After the Ice Age, the area around Perth was settled by Mesolithic hunter-gatherers. The standing stones and circles of Neolithic farmers are in abundance in the region. Stretches of Roman road can still be found and forts were built at the mouths of some of the big glens. There was a string of signal stations along the Gask ridge south-west of the town and a fort at Bertha, where the River Almond joins the Tay, two miles above today's Perth.

There is a local tradition that, when the Romans first looked down on what is now Perth, they claimed that it was just like Rome, and what we now think of as the North Inch was like the Campus Martius, or Mars Field. (It is very doubtful if any Roman who happened to be near Perth had ever been to Rome; but this is folklore!)

Sir Walter Scott liked to head up each chapter with a short quotation:

'Behold the Tiber,' the vain Roman cried,

Viewing the ample Tay from Baiglie's side;

But where's the Scot that would the vaunt repay,

And hail the puny Tiber for the mighty Tay!

At Scone, 2 miles north of Perth, Cinead, son of Alpin (as we must now call the Kenneth mac Alpin of my youth) brought together Scots and Picts to form Alba. At Luncarty, 5 miles north of Perth, the Danes were driven out. In 1210, William the Lion sealed the charter that made Perth a Royal Burgh.

Edward I, the Plantagenet, having conquered Wales and secured it with a string of castles, determined to make Scotland his own and almost did. As an expression of his domination, he had the Stone of Scone, or Stone of Destiny, taken to London, where it was fitted into a wooden chair. By the Treaty of Northampton (1328), England agreed to return the stone to Scotland, but riotous crowds prevented its removal from Westminster Abbey.

As a gesture, however, on Christmas Day 1950, four Scottish students removed the stone from the abbey and concealed it from the police search until returning it to the care of the Church of Scotland in Arbroath Abbey—where the Declaration of Arbroath was signed in 1320. As a gesture designed to stifle the growing tide of nationalism in Scotland, the stone was returned to Scotland, with some military ceremonial, in 1996.

Edward again, in 1304, ordered stone walls to be built around Perth. In 1313, Perth was recaptured and the walls destroyed, only to be rebuilt in 1336. Perth was a favourite residence of the early Stewart monarchs. Robert I ('the Bruce') had been the hero-king, brave, clever and eventually successful.

Robert II (1324-1371) and Robert III (1337-1406), father and son, 'had neither the personal qualities nor the prestige to command much respect', but on Palm Sunday 1396, the latter presided over a bloody affair which was to form the climax of one of Sir Walter Scott's novels.

Briefly, a dispute between Clan Chattan and Clan Kay was resolved by a thirty-a-side battle to the death on the North Inch of Perth. This would be a great sight to see, grandstands were erected and the King attended, no doubt to observe fair play at the judicial combat.

The Fair Maid of Perth was the first novel Scott wrote after his financial disaster and is considered to have been the best. It was written in four months and netted Scott £4,000 (c£400,000 today), and he retained the royalties. At one level, this is a good historical novel with a happy ending, but Scott chose to make it also a study of courage and cowardice.

On the North Inch, the fighting went on all day until only one of Clan Kay was left on his feet. Rather than die a glorious death, he ran to the river's edge, threw himself in and swam to the other side. Swimming the mighty Tay took some courage, if not desperation, and 'He who fights and runs away, lives to fight another day!'; sensible decision, heroic in its own way.

'Hal o' the Wynd', a Perth blacksmith, made up the numbers for Clan Chattan, fought mightily and killed seven of his opponents. The Black Douglas offered him a knighthood and a hundred-pound land with which to maintain it. The epitome of the surly Scot, Hal declined the offer, in words that became proverbial in Scotland: 'I fought for my own hand', meaning that he had done such a thing for his own pleasure, not for profit and certainly not to gain favour from one of the great ones of the land.

Scott also observes the behaviour of the King, Robert III. Halfway through the combat, he says: 'For God's sake, for the sake of the mercy which we daily pray for, let this be ended'. His brother, the Duke of Albany (fresh from the mysterious death of the King's eldest son, Rothesay, at Falkland), insists that the battle must go on. The King says:

You compel me to a great crime, Albany, both as a king, who should protect his subjects, and as a Christian man, who respects the brother of his faith.

And then:

I can but turn away and shut my eyes from the sights and sounds of a carnage which makes me sicken. But well I know that God will punish me even for witnessing this waster of human life.

After the battle the King made sure:

that care should be taken for the bodies and souls of the few wounded survivors, and honourable burial rendered to the slain, and secluded himself in his castle at Rothesay.

Perth was a favourite place from which Robert's son, James I, ruled his kingdom—and it was to be his last, as he was murdered on 21 February 1437 in the Dominican friary in Perth.

In 1554, five 'protestants' were burnt in Perth, and Perth's place in the history of Scotland was assured on 11 May 1559 when, in a frenzy of destruction, the mob 'cast doun' and destroyed everything in the main church of Perth that smacked of Popery—windows, statues and 'graven images'.

For many centuries, the plan of Perth changed little. Perth Bridge has always been of vital importance, to the town and to the country. But the Tay is a mighty river and it and the bridge have seen many a battle. Agricola is supposed to have thrown a wooden bridge across the Tay.

In October 1210, an ancient stone bridge was swept away. Another bridge was repaired in 1329 and it, or a replacement, was damaged in 1573, 1582 and 1589. Temporarily repaired with timber, it was entirely rebuilt in stone between 1599 and 1617, only for it to be 'finally demolished by a flood' in 1621. For well over a century, communication between the banks of the mighty river was by ferry, not often a swift and reliable mode of transport.

John Smeaton (1724-1792) was born in England of Scottish ancestry and can best be described as a professional inventor. His bridge (of 1771) was and is 'noble and elegant' as well as eminently practical. Widened in 1869-71, it is still a main crossing point of the Tay (the much later Queens Bridge of 1960, which replaced the Victoria Bridge of 1902, downstream takes a greater volume of traffic), and is an essential component of the national communications network.

The new bridge rejuvenated the city. In 1776, the city walls were demolished. Developments in the classical mode resulted in new public buildings and elegant terraces facing on to the North Inch and the South Inch.

Another force for change was the coming of the railway as part of 'the feverish building activity that had followed the mass of railway legislation of 1845'. The Dundee and Perth Railway opened to the east bank of the Tay opposite Perth in 1847. In 1849, the Tay was bridged, the extension to Perth Station causing havoc to the Georgian terraces. Dundee, via Perth, was now linked to the national railway network.

In 1848, the Scottish Central Railway reached Perth from south of Larbert. There was now a continuous rail link to and from London for the first time. An interesting beneficiary of this was Queen Victoria who, for some years, travelled by rail to Perth, stayed overnight at the Royal George Hotel, and then proceeded to Balmoral by coach over the hills to Glenshee, Braemar and Balmoral, her Deeside home. Later, she was able to make the through journey to Aberdeen and change to the Great North of Scotland line to Ballater.

By the end of the century, Perth was a real railway town, with the depots of three railway companies. From Perth, you could travel eight different routes. Perth could now really benefit from its strategic location and expanded rapidly.

For example, in 1937, Charles Oakley published *Scottish Industry Today,* 'A Survey of Recent Developments undertaken for The Scottish Development Council'. He described Pullars of Perth as one of the best-known firms in Great Britain, whose works were 'claimed to be the largest and best equipped cleaning and dyeing works in the world'. All dependent on the railway.

Pullars had agents in every town in the country, where laundry was taken in and sent to Perth, where it was processed and returned by rail the next day. The main platform at Perth, the second longest in Scotland, was quite a sight to be seen with rows of giant hampers of hotel linen queuing up for the appropriate train.

Perth was the market town for a large area of productive agriculture, and around the railway grew a large area of sidings and markets. In the years after World War 2, the beef barons of Argentina embarked on a campaign of improving their herds, until then only fit for corned beef. The annual Perth sales of Aberdeen Angus and Shorthorn bulls, for several years, attracted buyers from overseas and for a time world record prices were paid. The hotels did well too!

Although, Perth had now many of the characteristics of a regional capital as well as a county town, it suffered most of the characteristics of the decline in the British economy after 1945. Textiles have gone, as a result of conservative management and foreign competition. Social change, in the shape of a washing and drying machine in every home, killed the 'largest and best equipped cleaning and dyeing works in the world'. Dr Beeching's rail reforms closed half of the lines into Perth and killed the freight traffic.

The biggest 'white-collar' employer, the General Accident Insurance Company, was first taken over by a French company and then quietly tapered away. Many local enterprises have been taken over or shaded out by national and international chains. Yet, it is still a good place in which to live, with many attractions for the visitor, resident or passing through.

Despite not having a medieval cathedral, or a dominant castle, Perth has a very definite character which makes it well-known at home and abroad. But there is a problem and occasional confusion. There is another Perth, which some might say is even better-known than Perth, Scotland. In fact, as well as Perth, Western Australia, there is Perth in Tasmania.

There are 7 Perths in the United States; there have been 3 HMAS Perths in the Australian Navy. The Canadian Army once had a Perth Regiment. There is an asteroid called 3953 Perth, and the oldest surviving wooden boat in Western Australia is the MV Perth. So many Perths, some well-known in their own way.

One of the Australian Perth's main characteristics is its isolation. Today, it is one of the most isolated major cities in the world. The nearest city with a population of over 100,000 is Adelaide, 2,100Km (1,500 miles) away and separated by hundreds of miles of desert and semi-desert. Jakarta, capital of Indonesia, at 3,000Km (1,650 miles) is closer to Perth than Sydney, Brisbane or Canberra.

In the era of sailing ships, it was the Dutch who first used the Roaring Forties to sail directly from their colony at the Cape of Good Hope to the west coast of Australia, the first recorded sighting of the area being on 10 January 1697 by

Captain Willem de Vlamingh and his crew. The area looked inhospitable, and it was not until 1826 that—fearful of French annexation of the area—a convict-supported settlement was established by the Colony of New South Wales south of where Perth was to develop.

On 4 June 1829, the first British colonists sailed up the Swan River to found the town of Perth. A tree was ceremoniously cut down and Captain James Stirling, the Lieutenant Governor, proclaimed the establishment of the colony. From his name, Stirling must have been a Scot and he was carrying out the wish of Sir George Murray, in 1829 Secretary of State for the Colonies and Member of Parliament for Perthshire, to have the new settlement named in his honour.

The Swan River Colony was officially designated Western Australia in 1832. There were difficulties with the local Aboriginal people, who had been there for some 38,000 years and, unsurprisingly, resented their lands and customs being taken over by the white invaders.

Western Australia grew slowly and in 1850, it was opened to convicts as a source of cheap labour for the farming and business interests. In 1852, Perth was awarded city status by Queen Victoria—earlier than 'Old' Perth by the Tay! A gold rush in the 1890s was an early indication of the enormous mineral wealth of the state.

In 1901, the six colonies were federated into the Commonwealth of Australia, Western Australia being the most reluctant. One of the concessions offered to bring them in was the construction of the transcontinental railway across the Nullarbor Plain, linking Perth with the eastern cities. Perhaps because of its isolation from the other states the relationship has been occasionally edgy.

In 1933, Western discontent rose to a head and in a referendum, a large majority voted for secession. Eighteen months of negotiation, lobbying and referral to Westminster, allowed the issue to run into the sand.

The World War 2 and the mid-1960s were turning points for Western Australia, resulting in rapid growth for Perth. Cheap air travel made Perth as accessible as Sydney or Melbourne. Japan and China were the main markets for the state's vast mineral resources, and were, in global terms, just round the corner.

Up until 1945, Perth's population was almost entirely Anglo-Celtic in ethnic origin. There is an official list of the 250 suburbs in Perth. The early and continuing settlement of Scots is seen in such names as Applecross, Armadale, Attadale, Dalkeith and Eglinton. In 2006, the largest ancestry groups in Perth were still English (28.6%), Irish (6.2%), Scottish (6.1%), and 25.6% Australian. There was also an influx of Italians, Greeks, Dutch, Germans and Croats, with cultural implications. 5,000 Jews came in from Eastern Europe and South Africa.

The gradual relaxation of the White Australia Policy from 1966 brought about increased migration from South-east Asia—Vietnam (refugees), Malaysia, Indonesia, Thailand, Singapore, China and India. During the 1980s and 1990s, the phrase 'packing for Perth' was applied to Afrikaners and Anglo-Africans who emigrated abroad, regardless of destination, feeling threatened by changes in their country,

Perth, with 2 million of a population, is clearly a dynamic and attractive place in which to settle. What evidence is there for this? Perth came 7th in the Economist Intelligence Unit's August 2016 list of the world's most liveable cities, and was classified by the Globalisation and World Cities Research Network in 2010 as a world city. Perth is big, bustling and attractive, in an outward looking country.

Whatever we think in Scotland, for most people in the world, 'Perth' equals 'Perth, Australia' and our Perth is an ailing shadow of its booming, bustling namesake.

Nobody knows this better than the Postmaster of Perth, whose life is taken up with confusion and the misdirection of mail addressed to one Perth and delivered to the other or vice versa. At one time, there were amusing stories about the terrible mistakes being made, but we would suppose that, with the introduction of postcodes, ambiguities could not occur.

Not at all, it seems that the British postcode system cannot recognise the Australian system. When I discussed this with the Perth Delivery Line Manager, he walked out of the office and the first letter he picked up was for Western Australia. Ten per day is the average. When I expressed surprise at this, I was reminded that they handle 100,000 items daily!

One in ten thousand doesn't seem to be a worrying proportion, but it gives Perth, Scotland, a twist other cities do not share.

The Trail

Perth is such an ancient and vibrant city that any number of themes and trails could be followed. I have chosen to make this a Patrick Geddes Trail because Patrick Geddes (1854-1932)—biologist, town planner, re-educator, peace-warrior—was brought up here, receiving a solid grounding and inspiration for a career, which led him to become a world figure still respected by many today. By following this Patrick Geddes Trail, the enthusiast will also be acquiring a good understanding of how the city has developed.

The location of the numbered points on the trail is based on Roland PA Smith's *Perth Street Plan 2nd Edition*.

1. Wellshill Cemetery (H5)

Geddes was a man full of mysteries and contradictions, so it is fitting that we start with a touch of mystery in Geddes's background.

The main entrance to the cemetery is at the junction of Feus Road and Jeanfield Road. Do not use this. Instead go north along Feus Road, till you come to a side gate. Turn in here and take the road that leads to the right. Climb the steps on the left, turn right and after 20 metres, at E, turn left and follow the line of stones on the left.

As the slope flattens off, look left (east) where you can see, between two trees, a needle-like stone. The Geddes stone has its back to us, but is 5 metres from the track in the direction of the pyramid.

The Geddes stone is a fairly plain sandstone block. It says it was:

> Erected by Captain Geddes and Janet Stevenson, his wife, in memory of their beloved and only daughter
> Jessie who died 20 May 1884, aged 46
> Janet Stevenson or Geddes born at Airdrie 18 January 1816, died 26 February 1888
> Captain Alexander Geddes died 17 August 1899, aged 90

Captain Geddes? It says so on the stone. Twice. And this is corroborated by his death certificate and obituaries in the *Perthshire Courier* and three other local papers.

Yet Geddes was never a captain. How do we know?

  a) 31/3/1878 Service Record of Alexander Geddes. This is a printed form summing up A. G's career. The rank 'Captain' is scored out

and 'Quartermaster' written in twice. Below comes the following: 'I do certify that to the best of my knowledge and belief this statement is in all respects correct and true'. It is signed 'A Geddes QuMaster'.
   b) Census Perth 1861: 'Alexander Geddes, Aged 52, Chelsea Pensioner, Quarter Master Perthshire Militia'.
   c) A decorator's bill; now in the National Library of Scotland, was addressed to Captain Geddes. This was scored out by Alexander, who signed himself 'Lieutenant'.

Who are we to believe? Who gave the registrar and the newspaper reporters the 'facts'? (and there are another four definite errors of fact in these documents). Probably Anna Morton, his daughter-in-law over from Edinburgh, who nursed him at the end. Who told the stonemason what to cut into the stone? Probably Alexander, who knew pretty well that he was not a captain.

Was this a nickname? Possibly mocking some self-importance? Or is some underlying grudge coming out into the open?

Yes, it is all a mystery and one which is unlikely to be resolved.

Thoughtfully, we move on to Atholl Street and the North Inch through a zone of unremarkable post-industrial development of what used to be railway sidings, stockyards and the Black Watch barracks.

2. **Perth Academy** (K5) is the classical centrepiece of the elegant Rose Terrace, part of the early 19th century 'New Town' beyond the city walls. It was built in 1807 at a cost of about £7000.

Patrick did quite well at school without trying particularly hard. He won several prizes and left having achieved university entrance. While still at school, he was proposed for the Perthshire Society for Natural Science by Carl Fleckstein, his Modern Languages teacher. A year later (at 17), he was voted on to the Library Committee, which ensured special access to the Society's big and up-to-date collection.

'How are the mighty fallen'! The old academy is now the home of such as Handelsbank.

As we move round the edge of the North Inch, we cannot fail to be impressed by the view across the Tay and the survival of this urban lung as a place of recreation and entertainment—from clan battles in the past to the more homely football and cricket of today.

3. **Prince Albert Statue** (K5) was unveiled by Queen Victoria on 30 August 1864, three years after his death. It is a perfectly decent full-length figure, although it is beginning to show its age. The unveiling was a big event for Perth and the operation was masterminded by Alexander Geddes of the Perthshire Rifles.

He and the Queen had a special relationship, in that he had been headhunted to supervise the renovation of Balmoral in the 1850s. Young Patrick was 10 at the time of the unveiling, and one wonders about the chat around the breakfast table; did Alexander reminisce about what he said to Albert? Or what the Queen said he must do? Did she recognise him on the great day? Or did she maintain the stiff upper lip?

The inscription on the base of the statue reads 'Albert'. No more was needed in the 19th century. How might the youth of today respond: 'Albert? Who he?'

Cross the road and turn up right to the North Port (the North Gate, the limit of the medieval town).

4. **The Fair Maid's House** (K5)

The little group of houses are the oldest surviving houses in Perth. Sir Walter Scott knew this and made one the home of the 'Fair Maid' Catherine Glover. (Gloves were one of Perth's main products in pre-industrial times). The houses are much restored but, as the house agents say, 'with many original features', such as the grotesque above the niche at the south end. On page 156 of my copy of 'The Fair Maid', Scott is somewhat equivocal:

In Curfew Row, there is an old tenement, formerly the Glovers' Hall, and now pointed out as the house of Simon Glover, father of the 'Fair Maid'.

Some of the action of Scott's novel takes place in 'The Fair Maid's House' and one of the most beautiful tenor arias in the repertoire is sung in Bizet's *The Fair Maid of Perth* beneath Catherine's window. These tenuous connections have probably saved these fine buildings from 'redevelopment'. Instead, they have found new life as the Fair Maid Visitor Centre and the headquarters of the

Royal Scottish Geographical Society (established 1884), to whose magazine Patrick Geddes was a powerful contributor.

Take a short cut through Castle Gable and redeveloped Perth to Bridge Lane.

5. Perth Museum and Art Gallery (K5)

A splendid complex of buildings built around Marshall's Monument of 1824, with its great rotunda based on the Pantheon of Rome. For long, the home of the Museum of the Literary and Antiquarian Society and the Perth Library, it was greatly enlarged in 1932 when a new wing was opened by TRH The Duke and Duchess of York (better known to my generation as George VI and Queen Elizabeth, later the Queen Mother).

On my most recent visit, there was a temporary exhibition of hundred and fifty years of the Perthshire Society for Natural Science, of which Patrick Geddes was an active member (and who featured in the exhibition, along with some of his patrons) and was appointed librarian (at 17!).

In the bowels of the museum, safe from the public, are Geddes's Fair Book (of Mathematics) and his Merit Certificate of the Scotch Education Department.

Also, in a place of honour on the ground floor, are three fine portraits by Sir John Everett Millais, one of which displays a handsome Lady Millais (formerly Effie Gray), of whom later.

Now go up and over the approach to Perth Bridge. Go downstream and look back and appreciate the mighty Tay and its splendid bridge.

6. Smeaton's Bridge (K5-6)

Designed by John Smeaton in 1771, with eight elegant arches with cutwaters on the bridge piers and fine spandrels above. The bridge revolutionised transport in the east of Scotland and triggered the growth of Perth. It was widened to cope with increased traffic in 1869-71, and still is a vital part of the communications network—supplemented by the much later Queen's Bridge downstream.

It has weathered well, although you will note that the sandstone at the western end has resistant nodules of metamorphic rock sitting proud of the sandstone, which also shows the current bedding we associate with dune formation.

Now go upstream under the bridge and through the arch. Note the dated marks indicating the level of former floods. In the 19th century, the worst were in 1814, 1853, 1847, 1894. In the 20th century, the worst were in 1962, 1950, 1990, 1931, 1993. 2006 was another bad year.

1993 was catastrophic, but it was not the worst. That distinction belongs to 1814—but, of course, there was less of Perth to destroy then!

Lines marked XVIII and LXVII indicate feet above a certain level, but what level could it be? High Water Level Ordinary Spring Tides?

Now go back downstream.

7. Flood Prevention (K6)

After 1993, something had to be done and we can now see the results of massive investment. There are great metal barriers that can be swung into place when floods threaten. A massive new wall protects Tay Street from the river.

But Perth is a gracious town and has not allowed itself to be brutalised by these great engineering works. The black metal dams are camouflaged by panels of silvery metal with plant and animal stencils. In the concrete walls are niches with symbols, fruits or animals, and names of places and people, like Unthank and Douglas, or coats of arms, as with the twin town of Aschaffenburg.

There are sculptures. Salmon are prevalent, as they should be, the Tay being one of the best rivers of the world. On the great wall are interpretative plaques presented by the Guildry Incorporation of Perth, which received its Royal recognition in a Charter of 1210.

Look across Tay Street to the Royal George Hotel, a fine combination of the traditional and the modern. As an interesting example of the hazards of travel in early Victorian times, Queen Victoria intended to travel back to London from Balmoral by sea. But stormy weather kept her in Montrose till, on 29 September 1848, she got the new-fangled train to Perth and the Royal George. Next day, she continued her journey south by train from Perth.

In the hotel lounge are the lamps made from the four-poster bed in which she slept and the large 'By Appointment' which used to hang outside the hotel.

8. The Free Middle Church (K5-6)

Just below the hotel is what used to be the Free Middle Church. A fine Gothic sandstone building, with good windows and grotesques, and sittings for 830, it is now subdivided into residences. A photograph of 1890 shows the 43 heavily-bearded men of the Kirk Session outside the church hall, among them Alexander Geddes.

In 1843, 470 ministers and elders of the Church of Scotland walked out of the General Assembly in Edinburgh, and out of their manses and livings, on the issue of patronage. They set up the Free Church of Scotland, which was to have a strong intellectual influence on Scotland in the 19th century. In 1900, it absorbed the United Presbyterian Church to become the United Free Church, and finally merged with the established Church of Scotland in 1929.

Geddes's parents were strong adherents of the Free Church. His father was an Elder and helped organise the transfer of the congregation to this building in 1890. (The family tradition is that John McKail Geddes, Patrick's elder brother by ten years, fled to New Zealand to avoid being pressed into the ministry.)

The routine for this old couple on a Sunday was to walk down the hill, cross the bridge and attend the morning service. Thereafter, they would walk to the North Inch and eat their sandwiches (no cooking or any work on the Sabbath) before getting back to the 3 pm service and, ultimately, the long trudge back up to Mount Tabor.

Patrick Geddes was not a believer but did say that 'the institution with the greatest influence on me was the Free Church of Scotland'.

Proceed down Tay Street, developed at the height of Perth's prosperity in the 1880s. On the left is the river, and on the right is a potpourri of consciously handsome Victorian architecture. Every style of civic and ecclesiastical Gothic is there, broken up, unsurprisingly, by the massive Doric columns of Perth Sheriff Court. Well down the street, just beyond Canal Street, at 66, is a large Gothic building, now in multiple use.

9. The Perthshire Society of Natural Science Museum (K6)

In 1895, Robert Pullar (of 'Pullars of Perth') donated the site and much of the building costs for the PSNS Museum, lecture hall and library. On close inspection, as evidence of its original purpose, the capitals of the columns on either side of the door are ornamented with birds, flowers and leaves, while the letter box on the front door still bears the word 'Museum'.

While he lived in Perth, Geddes attended every meeting and field trip of the Society, and in later years, returned frequently to lend his support on important occasions and, it must be said, to seek sponsorship for his latest enterprise. The collection passed to Perth Town Council in 1902 and items still feature in the City Museum.

Cross the road and turn upstream to the Queen's Bridge, noting on the left more wavy metal seats protected by a metal windbreak with salmon cut-outs. Cross the bridge on the downstream side, noting once again the mighty river. Just before the traffic lights, go through the arch which says 'Rodney Gardens' and proceed downhill for about 50 metres to the prominent obelisk. Rodney Gardens is a good example of regeneration in that has been created on the site of a former mill.

10. Evergreen (K6)

The 'Evergreen' was the title of a periodical floated by Geddes in 1895, and an appropriate name for Kenny Munro's sculpture of 1998. It is a tribute to Geddes's mantra of Folk, Work and Place, expressing awareness of the natural world and the importance of the arts in education and community development.

In true Geddesian style, the sculpture has elements in words and symbols.

On top is a bronze seed or bud symbolising growth.

The fleur de lys reflects Geddes's love of France.

The elephant reminds us of his years spent planning in India.

His three doves could be Peace or his 'action-triad' of Sympathy, Synthesis and Synergy.

Juniper, Scots pine and laurel are, of course, our native evergreens.

A leaf reminds us that 'By leaves we live'.

The butterfly, flower and sun remind us of the fundamental processes of metamorphosis and photosynthesis.

The Tree of Life is a sacred symbol in many cultures.

Fittingly, Kenny's Geddes Pillar is now illuminated with special floodlights!

Come out by that same gate as in you went, turn right, cross Dundee Road, turn right and after about 100 metres, turn left into Manse Road. Climb to the roundabout and go straight ahead along, what is now, Mount Tabor Road. On the way up, you will pass first through big Victorian sandstone villas and then the more tightly packed, but still desirable, post-1945 homes. As the road narrows, you will see the stone-built Gean Tree Cottage.

11. Mount Tabor Cottage (M5?)

Much altered and extended, this was the home of the Geddes family for about fifty years, although it has been known as Gean Tree Cottage (gean = wild cherry = Prunus avium) for at least another fifty years. On the gable end is a small plaque informing us that Patrick Geddes spent his childhood in this cottage, from 1857 to 1874, and that he found in the Tay Valley and on Kinnoull Hill much inspiration for his life's work.

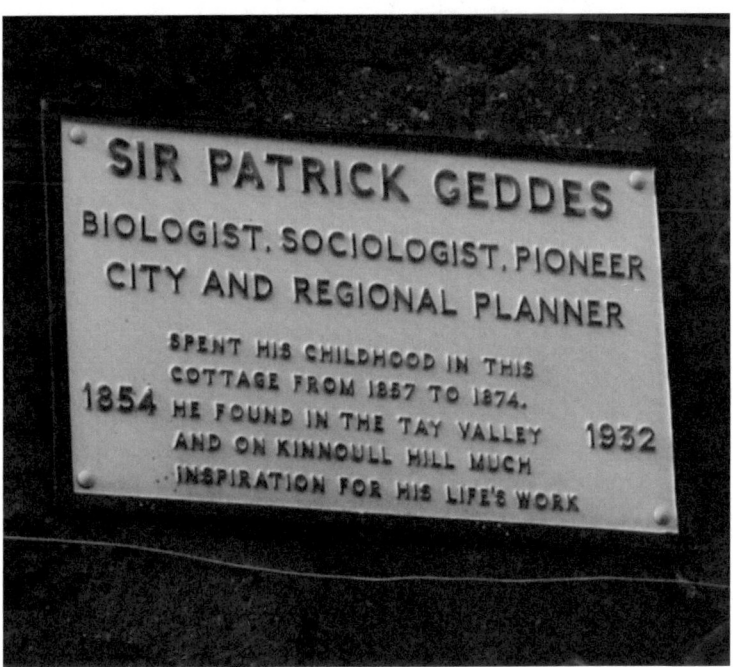

Fig 17: Patrick Geddes plaque, Mount Tabor

Fig 18:
Clan Geddes at Mount Tabor, 1912
(Alex Geddes)

At the 1861 census, this house had 6 windowed rooms and 7 residents—Alexander Geddes and his wife, their four children, three male, one female and a live-in servant. Even in 1861, this was overcrowding. There was no running water; water came from a well just inside the garden gate. Behind the cottage, the small stone building was the 'wash-hoose', the little chimney showing that there was a big copper in which the clothes were given the treatment.

In Geddes's time, on the Sabbath, the big garden was inspected and the next week's work planned.

Continue up the hill (pedestrians only) across Langley Drive and up a leafy lane, through modern villas to a metalled road and Corsiehill car park. Turn right and climb to the viewpoint and car park for Kinnoull Hill Woodland Park.

12. Kinnoull Hill (N6-7)

An information board ties Kinnoull Hill Woodland Park in with the Perthshire Big Tree Country. A good map sets out the various ways, trails, paths and loops available for all abilities, and we are told what to find and see. From here, we are told that it takes thirty minutes to reach the top of Kinnoull Hill. Looking outward is a grand panorama over Perth and the Tay, with the Highland Edge beyond. Behind is the wooded hillside.

The board features Patrick Geddes and quotes from him. ('By living we learn, by leaves we live'.) As a tease, we are told that one of his other famous phrases is carved into a bench on the summit of Kinnoull Hill. I will not spoil the fun by giving the answer—far better for you to find out for yourself!

Here, long before there were car parks and woodland parks, the young Geddes rambled, played and collected for the little museum his father had knocked together for him. This must be where the concept of the Valley Section had its birth. Perhaps you, too, can feel a little of the inspiration Geddes must have felt at this point.

Retrace your steps to the roundabout just below Mount Tabor Cottage. Turn down Bowerswell Road, steep and narrow. On the right, you will notice a cast iron horse trough for the poor animals grinding their way up the hill. Note also the handrail on the steepest portions. We can picture the young Geddes clattering down the hill in his kilt and tacketty boots on an icy morning on the way to the academy. No school run for him! (We have photographs showing this was everyday dress for him).

Angle back up right along the private road and between the gate posts of Bowerswell Memorial Homes Ltd. Bowerswell House is another splendid Victorian sandstone villa, with extensive modern additions. In the 19th century, it was the home of the Grays and the locus for a famous scandal, which must have had some interest for Geddes, and possibly some influence. Outside the house is a memorial stone which commemorates its 20th century purpose.

BOWERSWELL MEMORIAL HOMES

In thanksgiving for fifty years of peace and in remembrance of those who gave their lives in the War of 1939-45 to achieve that peace.

VICTORY IN EUROPE 8 MAY 1945
VICTORY OVER JAPAN 20 AUGUST 1945
Patrick Geddes, the Peace Warrior, would have approved.

13. Bowerswell (L5)

Effie (Euphemia) Gray (1828-1897) was a beautiful and well brought up young woman. John Ruskin was a very influential writer and critic, whose revolutionary *Modern Painters* was published in 1843. He fell for Effie and they were married in Bowerswell in 1848. (Ruskin's grandfather had killed himself there by cutting his own throat in 1817).

In 1848, Effie modelled for the painter Millais and there developed a 'love triangle'. Effie left her husband and filed for an annulment, on the grounds that the marriage had not been consummated. It may be that the reality of his wife's body did not match Ruskin's idea of perfection.

Millais and Effie were married in Bowerswell in 1855. There were eight children of the marriage. Millais prospered as a painter. Under Effie's influence, he became very rich and popular, was knighted in 1885 and made President of the Royal Academy in 1896—the year of his death. Effie shuttled between her childhood home and London—to the not quite highest society.

All of this was really juicy stuff, given plenty publicity by a prurient press and Queen Victoria refused to have either of the couple in her presence, until, when Millais was dying, Princess Louise persuaded her mother to allow Effie to attend an official function.

The Geddeses were well below the Grays in the Mount Tabor pecking order and it is unlikely that they even met. Patrick was born in the year the marriage to Ruskin was annulled (1854) but, as he grew up, there would be lots of telling and retelling of the unsavoury goings on down the road. As part of his 'home studies', Geddes went to art classes in Perth's Art College.

He not only read Ruskin but formed many of his ideas from him. When at the Royal School of Mines in 1875, he took a month out to visit the museums and galleries of London. In 1887 and 1888, he had the confidence (or cheek?) to write substantial (over 50 pages) essays on *Every Man His Own Art Critic* for exhibitions in Manchester and Glasgow.

While not an artist in the conventional sense Geddes did have a talent for didactic visual representation, often in the form of 'thinking machines', which might pass for art in our colleges today. He could be considered an art patron in that, in his various civic operations, he commissioned decorative and instructive glass panels, sculptures, paintings, murals, ceilings, a Witches' Well, often in Celtic Revival style.

Critical of Edinburgh College of Art, he set up his own School of Art in a former Ragged School adjacent to the Outlook Tower, with John Duncan as principal. Under-capitalised, of course, like most of his enterprises.

Geddes must have known at least one of Effie's children, John ('Johnny') Guille Millais (1865-1931), also known as 'The Ornithologist'. He was born in Annat Lodge, the fourth son and seventh child as Effie's family overflowed into the next villa. He had the wanderlust. After six years in the Seaforth Highlanders, he travelled over several continents hunting, shooting, collecting and painting birds and plants.

He co-founded the Society for the Preservation of the Wild Fauna of the Empire and was taken into the Secret Service in 1914. He wrote 17 books, including biographies of his father and FC Selous, the greatest big game hunter of his day. His son recalled a chaotic busy house and a father who was 'enormously intelligent, with the energy of a racing car, a workaholic with immense enthusiasm and a keen sense of the ridiculous'.

Millais' main residence was in Sussex but he was a frequent visitor to Perth, and was an active member of the Perthshire Society of Natural Science. He and Geddes must have met on some of the occasions when the latter was revisiting the Society. They must have got on well together as they were both dynamic and with a bewildering array of interests.

The Trail completed, all that needs to be done now is to descend the hill and cross Smeaton's bridge to regain the Fair City of Perth.

Chapter Ten

Slaughter of the Innocents
Sir Andrew Murray and Dunblane

Sir Andrew Murray (to be known as Andy from this point on) is the greatest tennis player Britain has had since before World War 2, and probably the best in all time. At 3, he started on the local tennis courts in Dunblane, a modest but decent place near Stirling. At 8, he was competing with adults in the local Central League. At 15, he might have signed for Rangers, but decided to focus on tennis instead, going to Spain for eighteen months—'a big sacrifice' for his parents.

His coach at this time described him as 'unbelievably competitive'. Aged 18, he became the youngest Briton to play in the Davis Cup.

An elderly curmudgeon like myself is always grumbling about dastardly imports from America, particularly the US. 'Gotten' was taken over there by the early settlers, but has now made the return journey back, to the confusion of teachers. We no longer have skeletons in our cupboards, they are in our closets. Or perhaps hidden behind our drapes. We throw rocks at each other instead of stones.

Some US towns are well-known for the worst of reasons. In 1995, a bomb in Oklahoma City killed 168 people and injured over 680. The perpetrators were US citizens, one was executed and the other 2 imprisoned. The Columbine High School massacre of 1999 saw the deaths of 12 students and one teacher. The perpetrators, both US citizens, committed suicide.

The Virginia Tech shooting of 2007 was a solo effort by Seung-Hui Cho, a senior-level undergraduate of 23. Born in South Korea, he came to the US at the age of 8 and became a permanent resident. He rewarded the United States for its hospitality by being responsible for 32 deaths and committing suicide in the building where most of the killings took place.

At the Sandy Hook Elementary School, Connecticut in 2012, Adam Lanza shot and killed his mother, 20 school children, 6 teachers and then himself. In 1996, the year of Dunblane, there were 11 fatal shootings in US schools.

For these, and many other shootings, the response was the same. 'Something must be done'. There were petitions and condolences, tributes and vigils. President Obama twice wiped away tears in a television address after Sandy Hook.

Yet, when a white man entered the Emmanuel African Methodist Episcopal Church in Charleston, South Carolina, and slew 9 unarmed worshippers, 'in hopes of igniting a race war', the National Rifle Association spokesman blamed the victims, saying that, if they had carried arms, they would have been able to drive off the killer. And so the story goes on.

On the surface, the Dunblane massacre looked as if it might be the offspring of this American habit. On 13 March 1996, Thomas Hamilton (43), a local man with a doubtful reputation and a grudge, armed himself with 4 legally-held handguns and 743 bullets, cut the school's telephone cables and entered the gymnasium. There, and outside a mobile classroom, he killed 16 children and the Primary One teacher, all in three minutes.

He re-entered the gym, where he would have seen the dead teacher and children, the wounded and terrified. He dropped the pistol he was using, and equipped himself with one of the two revolvers. He put the barrel of the gun in his mouth, pointed it upwards, and pulled the trigger, killing himself.

As in the United States, there was a vast outpouring of public and private grief and public debate, the outcomes of which were the Cullen Report, the passing of two new Firearms Acts and the effective banning of private ownership of handguns in Great Britain (but not Northern Ireland).

The judiciary came in for criticism as it emerged that Hamilton had been investigated in 1991 by the Child Protection Unit of Central Scotland and a report for consideration of ten charges, including assault, obstructing police and contravention of the Children and Young Persons Act 1937 had been passed to the procurator fiscal. No action had been taken. There were accusations of a cover-up: 'intended to protect the reputations of officials'.

There was a massive change in the way Scottish schools presented themselves to their community. Up until Dunblane, Scottish schools were developing an openness sadly lacking in over a century. From being grim places devoted to 'yark the learnin' in', they were becoming light, airy and welcoming.

Many secondary schools were transforming themselves into community schools, where adults and students could study together, or share swimming pools, PE and Outdoor Education facilities. In primary schools, parents were welcomed into the life of the school, actively as well as passively.

Almost overnight all of this changed. Fences, padlocks and security cameras proliferated. Access was controlled by key pads and passwords. At the same time, there was a concern about child safety and anyone likely to come in contact with children was subjected to security checks. Whatever Thomas Hamilton imagined he was doing in the Dunblane gym, he was certainly successful in ending, what some might say, was a 'touchy-feely' culture, and having it replaced by one of narrow suspicion of one's fellow-men, and women.

Although, an ancient place, Dunblane was never of great importance. In 1150, a bishopric was established, but just after the Reformation it was 'the poorest and smallest of Scotland's sees'. But it was a decent place, with a fine river, the Allan Water, which drove some mills and attracted, in the 19th century, an out-station of Pullars of Perth, 'the largest and best equipped cleaning and dyeing works in the world'.

Otherwise, it was like many a town on the fringes of the Highlands, a market place, with spinning mills and handloom weavers, for a time.

Paul Pry, Junior on 17 June 1847, wrote in the *Stirling Observer* about Bridge of Allan. His article would have applied equally well to Dunblane, 2 miles further north.

The Scottish Central Railway, now forming, will soon be completed, and then 'a' things will be right'. Only think, Sir, of the facility with which parties then may reach this watering-place, bringing, as it will bring, the cities of Edinburgh and Glasgow within little more than an hour's travel…Those who may yet travel by the Scottish Central, have a rich treat awaiting them in their descent from the north, for, after leaving behind them the moss hags and peat bogs of Blackford and Strathallan, they enter a beautiful glen…

Skirting 'Allan Water' the whole way, and crossing it several times the line is embosomed in hazel glades and hawthorn dales. Strange to say, few of the inhabitants of Stirling avail themselves of the privilege within their reach.

In 1848, the Scottish Central Railway came to Dunblane, and by 1865, it was part of the powerful Caledonian system, giving Dunblane direct access to the 'eight large towns' of Scotland, and even London! As a minor junction, it was the take-off point for the Callander and Oban Railway. By rail, Glasgow was a mere 34 miles away, and Edinburgh 41, making commuting a possibility for wealthy businessmen.

It probably did no harm that Kippendavie, the home of Patrick Stirling, Chairman of the Caley, was a mile outside Dunblane, and that he ensured the environment was undisturbed by having the railway pass through his land in a tunnel!

'A good many handsome villas and various public edifices' were the result. A mineral spring behind the cathedral was acquired by a limited company who built 'a fine hydropathic establishment, capable of accommodating 200 visitors' in 1875, at a cost of £22,000. In the shadow of the Dunblane Hydro, other hotels and boarding houses were set up, as were some small private schools.

The British public is notoriously forgetful of its responsibilities to those who fought for it, but in 1908 was established the Queen Victoria School, which partially relieved the national conscience by taking in and educating Scottish service children. Residential, co-educational from 1996, and funded by the Ministry of Defence, it became best known by its pipe band playing before and at half-time in Scottish internationals at Murrayfield.

Unfortunately, its reputation was tarnished by allegations of paedophilia in 1991, 2003 and 2005, and by the reluctance of the MOD and the legal establishment to handle the concerns openly.

In the 20th century, the Hydro continued to flourish, spawning off other hotels and guest houses. With the coming of the motor car, Dunblane eventually found itself one mile from the end of the main Scottish motorway network and commuter estates spread around the town. For most people, Dunblane was a good place to live—quiet, with pleasant walks and a tradition of gentility yet with all the facilities of a decent town and good transport links.

Then came the outrage of the massacre of little children and their teacher. How could Dunblane be unaffected? And how could the other children in the school that day, whether they were in the gym or not, be unaffected? Let us look at Judy Murray's two little boys, who were there, and who are now creating a very different image for Dunblane.

Judy Murray (née Erskine) was born in nearby Bridge of Allan in 1959. She was successful in Scottish tennis, turned professional in 1976, giving up when she was homesick and robbed in Barcelona. She went to Edinburgh University, and represented Britain at the 1981 World Student Games before taking up coaching.

She introduced her sons to the game at an early age and coached them until they were well up the rankings. It is only recently, however, that she has been able to stand back entirely from their game and carve out a new career in the promotion of tennis and the establishment of centres of excellence.

On the day of the massacre, Jamie's class would have been well away from the gymnasium. The action would have been heard but not seen. The class took cover, the sensible thing to do. Jamie (born 1986), in the year of Dunblane, was to become No 3 in Europe. At 13, he was the junior world number 2.

With four other boys, he was selected for training by national coaches at The Leys School, Cambridge, but, as the youngest, Jamie had to attend St Faith's, the feeder school down the road. He felt isolated, did not like the coaching and returned home after eight months. There, he did not touch a tennis racket for two years.

In 2004, he turned professional. He performed well enough, but lost his singles ranking in 2007. But, the same year, with Jelena Jankovic, he won the Mixed Doubles title at Wimbledon, the first Briton to win a title at Wimbledon for twenty years. From then on, he played with a variety of partners, winning two more Grand Slam titles in 2016 (Australian Open and US Open).

Also in 2016, Jamie became Doubles World No 2, while his brother was Singles World No 2. Later that year, Jamie became Doubles World No 1. In all, he has won 26 Major titles.

The brothers did not hit it off well in their earlier days, but in 2015, Jamie was brought into the British team for the Davis Cup final against Belgium, when the brothers won their doubles match. This was the first time Britain had won the cup for seventy-nine years. Jamie joined the rest of the Davis Cup team for the BBC Sports Personality of the Year Show, where they won the 2015 Team of the Year Award. In 2016, Jamie was awarded an OBE 'for services to tennis and charity'.

Commentators tend to look down their noses at doubles, and doubles matches seem to be fitted in to competitions as an afterthought. But the very best players do not always play at their best side by side. The essence of doubles is co-operation and understanding and two intelligent players can often humble the big guns.

Jamie was clearly not of the highest calibre on his own, but was able to read the doubles game and to work well with a range of partners; in fact his career was remarkable in that for most of it he had only one coach but over fifty partners.

Jamie's nickname is 'Stretch' (His height is 1.90m, or 6ft 3in.) As well as being tall, he is dark and moderately handsome. Being left-handed is probably helpful in a doubles partnership. He appears pleasant and open-tempered. The brothers now get on well together, although there were tensions in the past.

He has been spared close media attention, except when he had the temerity to marry a Colombian. To an outsider, there is little sign of trauma from the shooting incident.

Fifteen months younger than his brother, Andy seems a more complex character. His kneecap at birth was two separate bones, which did not fuse together as is normal. The result is intermittent pain. He has had to withdraw from competitions as a result.

He attended a youth group run by Thomas Hamilton, and his mother gave Hamilton lifts in her car. He is reticent about talking about the massacre, saying he was too young to understand what was happening. In fact, he hid under the teacher's desk, a very sensible thing to do. At the age of 10, his parents very messily divorced, leaving his mother a dominant force in his life.

Andy started at 3 on the local tennis courts. At 8, he was competing with adults in the local Central League. At 15, he might have signed for Rangers, but decided to focus on tennis instead, going to Spain for eighteen months—'a big sacrifice' for his parents. His coach at this time described him as 'unbelievably competitive'.

In 2005, Andy turned professional and, aged 18, became the youngest Briton to play in the Davis Cup. He also split from his coach—this was to become a frequent occurrence in the Murray Story. He had a tendency to build up his own inner circle of support and play them off against his coaches—ten of them over the years.

In 2006, he became Britain's No 1, ending Tim Henman's seven-year reign. At the same time, he was No 42 in the world. He was doing well, but there was a suggestion that he was not quite strong enough to make it to the top. By 2006, he was No 10 and in 2007, he made it to No 4. For several years, he bumped around the No 4 position.

He fell away badly due to back trouble, and underwent back surgery in 2013. He then fought his way back to No 2 in 2015. 2016 was a good year as he won a second Olympic gold, Wimbledon (for the second time) and seven other titles to reach world No 1 position. On his way to the top, Murray had picked up BBC Sports Personality of the Year in 2013 and 2015, and shared the 2015 Team of the Year Award. In 2013, his first Wimbledon year, he was also awarded the OBE.

Why did it take him so long? Why was he stuck so long at No 4? There are three answers—Roger Federer, Rafael Nadal and Novak Djokovic. For more than a decade, these wonderful players battled it out at the top and it looked as if Murray could never break through. They were almost the same age (Federer born 1981, Nadal born 1986, Murray born 1987, Dyokovic born 1987, one week after Murray), so it was unlikely that Murray could win by outlasting the others.

Federer was supremely elegant and never seemed to be hustled into errors. Djokovic was, quite simply, powerful. Murray had a hard time with each of them, over the years the results being as follows—Federer 14, Murray 11: Nadal 17, Murray 7: Djokovic 24, Murray 10. The struggles with Djokovic in particular were titanic; some of their matches have been described as the best tennis matches ever played, and most of us were resigned to thinking that Murray had done very well in becoming the best British player of the modern era—but that was as far as he could go.

However, 2016 turned out to be a great year for Murray. Federer was getting old and playing less frequently. Nadal's furious style of play had caught up with him, he broke down and then found a return to the game frustrating. Djokovic, after two years of total dominance, lost form, fell ill and struggled to reach the heights again. Murray finished the season in great style, winning a string of 24 matches in a row, and ending with a 6-3 6-4 win over Djokovic.

As *The Herald* said:

Dunblane's finest finishes the longest campaign of his life in style by sweeping Serb aside to remain atop rankings.

At the end of 2016, *The Herald* summed him up thus:

He has honed a ferocious work ethic and overcome crushing despair when results went against him. He has brought honour and distinction to his country and is an exemplar for society.

For the third time, Murray was voted BBC Sports Personality of the Year, showing a fine disregard for the honours system by declining to interrupt his training for the awards ceremony, accepting the trophy by video link at the poolside in Miami. On the last day of 2016, it was announced that he was to become Sir Andrew Murray, at 29, one of the youngest to be knighted in the modern era.

Clearly all four of these great players are superb tennis players. What marks Murray out from the others? He is reputed to be one of the most intelligent tacticians on the court. He is very mobile about the court, and is one of the best returners of the lightning serves of the best. He tends to defend on the baseline, making few errors.

Typically, he and his opponent batter away at each other for long rallies. The opponent then unleashes a certain winning shot which Murray first reaches, and then from somewhere releases a ferocious angled reply which leaves his opponent speechless. He 'may be the best counterpuncher on tour today'.

His spirit is indomitable. Time was when he would crumble in the midst of a game. Now he is a danger to public health, in that he twists the emotions of his supporters by his last-minute escapes. So often have we seen him 2-0 down and match point against him, only for him to win the crucial point and then fight his way back to win the match.

It has to be said that Murray is no poster boy. Although, he is the same height as his brother, Andy is scrawny when his brother is easy on the eye. His footwear always looks dull and clumsy. On the court, he frequently mouths and curses and shouts at the crowd. (It could well be that he is cursing his own ineptitude and abusing his coach, not the spectators). In victory he can throw back his head and give an animal roar which is really disturbing.

He is not comfortable with the media, preferring to play table games with his entourage to soft-soaping the public. In his early days, he could be sullen and sulky in interview. When he joked that he would support 'whoever England is playing' in the World Cup of 2006, he was vilified by those who compared him unfavourably with the emollient Tim Henman.

At the referendum time in 2014, he was subjected to 'vile' (the word used by the police) abuse, referring to the Dunblane massacre. He has been booed by feminists and fined for swearing at an umpire.

In a profession notorious for pussyfooting around, he has been outspoken on match-fixing and on the double standard of the media when his coach, Mauresmo (a woman), was blamed for his (temporary) loss of form. As he said: 'Have I become a feminist? Well, if being a feminist is about fighting so that a woman is treated like a man then, yes, I suppose I have'.

However, it is probably true to say that Murray won over the Great British Public by winning the Davis Cup for them, almost single-handed, by picking up the major honours of the game and, above all, by the sheer determination he has shown in his long march to the top.

With success, marriage and fatherhood, his gentler side has had a chance to show itself.

However, 2017 did not prove as successful as 2016. According to *The Herald*:

Murray is still paying the price for the superhuman run of tournament wins in late 2016 and his No 1 spot.

Early in the year, he suffered a string of minor but irritating injuries which resulted in some cancellations. Then, in the quarter-final at Wimbledon, a hip injury flared up and we found ourselves watching this poor soul hirpling hopelessly around the court, while his much less talented opponent walked away with the match. He did not play again that summer and worried his fans by not being able to meet the ferocious demands of the top tennis circuit.

Meanwhile, Nadal's knees had recovered; he was 'proudly back at the summit of the sport' and recovered the No 1 position. Federer had surgery on his knee in February 2016. He was now selective in the tournaments he entered for and was rewarded by picking up two majors, with apparently effortless arrogance and easing himself again into the No 1 slot. Of the Big Four, Djokovic developed an elbow problem and dropped out halfway through the summer season.

Murray, at the same time, underwent surgical operations and treatments, only to continue to disappoint. There was still something heroic about a former master who refused to give up and took on younger and fitter players—even though he could not proceed further than the second or third round.

However, late in 2022, we saw a rejuvenated Murray with metal reinforcements. With his old coach Lendl he began climbing up the rankings, in January 2023 playing in – and winning – the longest match of his career, which ended at 4 a.m.!

In this world, where alleged victims parade their every unsavoury experience for the media to publicise, can we assess the long-term effects of Hamilton's murder trip on the Murray boys, witnesses but not eye-witnesses? Do they now avoid the place, with its horrific memories, like the plague? A search engine gives Jamie's place of residence as 'Dunblane'.

(The same search engine gives Andy's place of residence as 'London', but, in fact, he spends most time, when not travelling, in Florida, because of the demands of the high-level tournament fixture list).

Jamie was married in a hotel just outside Dunblane (Andy was best man). The hotel has since been bought and upgraded by Andy. The town has recognised how lucky it is to have the Murray boys reshaping its image, and they are suitably keen to help with the rebuilding of this douce little town.

Jamie's behaviour on court seems more equable, while Andy can be like a sulky schoolboy—but is this any worse than the behaviour of certain other top players from trouble-free backgrounds? Whatever Jamie's emotions, he seems to have them well under control. Andy is reticent about this incident in the past but his occasional extravagant behaviour may be a means of harnessing his emotions at a crucial point in the game.

How can we assess the long-term effects on its survivors of such a childhood massacre? And how does Dunblane show how it has recovered?

The Trail

How significant in its history of a thousand years is Thomas Hamilton's crime? The purpose of this trail is to investigate the character of Dunblane, to lead the interested observer through the town and consider the evidence, not to wallow in morbid curiosity.

It is logical to start with the Allan Water at the **Faery Bridge.** The river is brawling and powerful, a real Highland river in a lowland setting. Its power was used to drive some 12 mills, the usual meal and corn mills, silk and woollen thread mills, even a mill which produced confetti!

Further upstream was Pullars' dyeworks. Just above the bridge were the mills of Wilson's of Bannockburn famous for their tartan cloth. They operated from 1853 till 1977, with workers' housing and, in the 19th century, with a school where the children worked half-time in the mill and went half a day to school. Now the buildings have been restored and gentrified.

Like most mill towns, there was an informal network of footpaths from the town down to the mills, used by the workers in the early mornings. Looking downstream from the bridge can be seen the mill dams and lades created to serve the various enterprises. The footpath network has been transformed into a series of riverside walks. On the left, a former quarry has been converted into a community garden.

The so-called Faery Bridge was built in 1911, replacing the wooden bridge which gave workers from the east side of the river direct access to the mills. You will notice that the bridge is built of ferro-concrete. It started life as the Ferro Bridge but gradually metamorphosed into the more romantic Faery Bridge!

We now go downstream, under the railway bridge, to the cathedral area, where we turn left, up the hill to **Dargai Terrace**, which is an excellent measure of urban change. On the left are sturdy stone Victorian/Edwardian two-storey villas, with a view over to the cathedral and the river and with large gardens sweeping downhill. On the right is an extensive post-World War 2 development of desirable villas, geared to the motor car, with small gardens and no view.

And Dargai? What is this? In 1897, the Afghan tribes on the north-west Frontier were getting troublesome and the Tirah Field Force was sent to sort them out. At Dargai, the force was blocked and battered away all day at trying to break through. At three in the afternoon, Colonel Matthias of the Gordon Highlanders said, 'The Gordons will clear the way', and sent the regiment to climb and clear the Heights of Dargai.

It did not prove too easy at first until Piper Findlater was wounded in both ankles. He crawled to his pipes, hitched himself up against a big boulder 'wi' the shots pingin' away round him', and began piping up the regimental march, whereupon 'the boys took heart and carried the crest', allowing the Field Force to advance on to Kabul.

As George MacDonald Fraser wrote in *The General Danced at Dawn*:

What he (Piper George Findlater) did on an Afghan hillside one afternoon caught the public imagination, as it deserved to, more than such things commonly do.

Today, we would say his exploit went viral. The empire needed a hero. Pictures were painted and prints made. 'Cock o' the North' was sounded up the length and breadth of the land, in music-halls, by brass bands and by street fiddlers. The butcher boys in the street whistled it and sang it to naughty words.

Findlater had been invalided back to Britain, and Queen Victoria travelled all the way from Windsor to Netley Military Hospital on Southampton Water to pin the Victoria Cross on the hero's breast.

What other name than Dargai could be given to a brand-new terrace of decent houses in a town that had provided some of those who stormed the Heights on that great day?

Back down now to **Dunblane Cathedral** surrounded by its graveyard, with something of the air of an English cathedral close. A cathedral is the seat of a bishop and, strictly speaking, Dunblane ceased to be a cathedral when, in 1559, the Earl of Argyll purged the building of 'all Kynd of monuments of idolatry'. The cathedral was stripped and the bishop was given his marching orders.

Fortunately, the building itself was spared and the church became, in effect, the parish church of Dunblane. For a small town like Dunblane, it was a big church to maintain, and it is now owned by Historic Scotland and is given the title of cathedral because of its origins.

Building started soon after 1237 and went through several phases, which can be worked out by inspection. On the south side is an awkwardly placed bell tower, with the upper part restored, whose masonry is palpably older than the main body of the cathedral. The church itself was reroofed and heavily restored in the 19th century, and consists of a choir and a nave, with fine windows. The great John Ruskin it was who addressed an Edinburgh audience:

Do you recollect the West window of your own Dunblane Abbey*? It is acknowledged to be beautiful by the most careless observer…He was no common man who designed that cathedral of Dunblane. I know nothing so perfect in its simplicity, and so beautiful…in all the Gothic with which I am acquainted.

*Oops!

Unusual for a Scottish church are the very fine 15th century carved wooden choir stalls and canopies above—spared by the Earl of Argyll!

As befits a Church of Scotland church, the interior is quite plain, but there are interesting monuments which tell us something about what makes Dunblane what it is. In the choir is the recumbent tomb of Bishop Clement (1233-58), the power behind the early growth of Dunblane. Near the good bishop is a commemorative plaque which appealed to me.

Rev Robert Napier, Intelligence Officer, The Nyasaland Field Force, who having served at Karonga in 1914 and in German East Africa in 1917, fell in action in Portuguese East Africa on 11 Feb 1918, aged 37 years.

Ordained in the Choir of this Cathedral 1909, a Missionary of the Church of Scotland and in Nyasaland, he had the high privilege of training the first members of the native ministry and of sharing in the translation of the Bible in Tonyanja.

Glasgow University added some detail, saying that, on the outbreak of war, he took part in the defence of Nyasaland, doing valuable service in charge of the native transport lines.

Later, he served with the native transport in German East Africa. His great linguistic attainments enabled him to take the post of Intelligence Officer to the British Force, and it was while attached as Lieutenant to the 4/1st King's Africa Rifles that he fell in Portuguese Africa on the 11 February 1918. Fearless and zealous in the cause of others, he had gone forward to reconnoitre the enemy's lines, when he fell mortally wounded. Robert Napier's loss can never be rightly estimated. 'His memory lives and inspires.'

Nyasaland is now Malawi, which still has a special relationship with the Church of Scotland and the Scottish government. Dr Hastings Banda, the first President of Malawi, studied medicine at Edinburgh (part-subsidised by the Church of Scotland), became an elder of the Church of Scotland, and worked as a doctor in Renfrew. He also had his dark side!

Off the choir is a memorial chapel commemorating Dunblane's local heroes (and heroines). Unusually, there is a Dunblane Cathedral Roll of Honour:

Which is a record of the Men who fought for their King and Country in the Great European War 1914-18.

In egalitarian alphabetical order. The corresponding World War 2 Roll of Honour is arranged alphabetically within Sea, Land and Air units. An interesting wooden plaque is headed up 1939-1945 and says:

> To the Glory of God
> In Memory of the Men and Women
> Who served unto Death
> And in Gratitude for those
> Who returned after Service and Suffering

Interesting attitudes.

On the north wall of the nave, there is an array of plaques recording the members of the House of Kippendavie from 1545 to 1859. These were put in place in 1892 by Patrick Stirling of Kippendavie, local laird and railway magnate, who was not only a financier and manager but a designer, his most famous locomotive being the Stirling 8ft single, so called because of the single 8ft driving wheel!

Around the west door is a collection of sculptured stones, rescued from the locality, including what is usually called a Pictish symbol stone.

Coming round to the south side of the nave is the white sandstone Standing Stone Commemoration, unveiled on 12 March 2000 (PLATE 7b). It is simple and pure with inscriptions on each side. One is RH Stoddard's *Children's Prayer*:

If there is anything that will endure the eye of God because it is pure it is the spirit of a little child.

Dignified, not vengeful.

Leave the cathedral now and look across to **Kirk Street,** a plain but satisfying assemblage of 18th century housing, until recently Scottish Churches House, but now privately owned and discreetly converted into a hotel, café, wine bar, brasserie. Look up to the left, up **Sinclair's Street**, and get a good impression of what a Scottish burgh street was like. On **Kirk Street** more modest burgh architecture.

Cross over to kirkyard wall—plaque marking spot of Tolbooth. Commemorative tree planted by HRH Princess Royal.

Go down side of Cathedral Hall (1997 and earlier pastiche of 17th century Renaissance architecture) to the remains of the **Bishop's Palace**, with an interpretation board by the children of Dunblane Cathedral Senior Sunday School, April to June 2015.

Return to The Cross and note Dunblane Museum, in a traditional 3-storey block with a forestair. Next comes a 2-storey house with forestair and then the Burgh Chambers with crow-stepped gables. Across the road is an impressive, but rather odd, building. It is a traditional 2½ storey block with a forestair, crow-stepped gables and an ornamental but empty cartouche on the main wall.

(This once held a marble tablet with the Bishop's arms and the inscription *Bibliotheca Leightoniana*). But it has very few windows. The lower end gives us a clue. It is a big blank wall with only a Venetian window but two ventilators in the top storey.

This building is the **Leighton Library**, which may be the oldest purpose-built library in Scotland. It was built c1680 to house the collection of Bishop Leighton, was a lending library in the 18th century, and is now administered by the University of Stirling. Although, bishops were abolished in 1560, they were re-introduced by James VI and Charles I, and again by Charles II.

The Scottish Episcopal Church now has 7 bishops, one of whom is Bishop of St Andrews, Dunkeld and Dunblane, whose cathedral is in Perth.

Next to the Leighton Library, the last building in old Dunblane, is the simple late Georgian Bank House of 1835, 63 High Street, which can be thought of as the first building in 'new' Dunblane. It was built for Charles McAra, Sheriff Clerk, famous for wearing gloves on his head to conceal his baldness.

Across the street, on the site of the old jail, is a nice **garden** with three modest features. A garden seat has a plate:

> Remembering the children who so tragically lost their lives
> from
> Friends at Lordswood Leisure Centre
> 1998

A little cairn quotes from John Milton in 1652: 'Peace hath her victory no less renowned than war'. And another plaque was placed there:

> In memory of the teacher and children who so tragically lost their lives on 13 March 1996
> Always remembered by the Burnt Oak, Edgware and Mill Hill community.

Looking across the roundabout, at the top of the High Street, you will observe a **pillar box**, painted gold (PLATE 8a). The plaque reads as follows:

> This post box has been painted gold by Royal Mail to celebrate
> **Andy Murray**
> Gold Medal winner
> London 2012 Olympic Games
> Tennis: Men's Singles

There is a fitting symbolism here. On one side of the road, on the edge of the historic core of Dunblane, we feel the melancholy of the murdered teacher and her pupils—but the sympathy of so many **strangers**—while, across the road on the fringe of the busy commercial heart, we celebrate the success of one who was present at the massacre but rose above the trauma. Well done, Dunblane!

Unfortunately, nothing relating to Andy Murray is ever simple. One day, a tourist parked his car on the street above the pillar box, forgot to put on the hand brake and walked away. The car rolled off down the hill, demolishing Andy's pillar box! Is there a moral to this tale, about the transience of fame? So, what we see today is Andy's pillar box Mark II.

For me, the rest of the trail is of lesser interest, but we must move on to the two main signature buildings. From the roundabout, turn up the hill, past the Court House of 1844—more like a fortress than the seat of justice—to a big roundabout, the old Perth road and a spread of decent and recent suburban villas.

Up on the right is, what I insist on still calling, the **Dunblane Hydro**. Built in 1875-76 at a cost of £22,000, it is superbly and arrogantly set on the brow of the hill, looking across to the Highland Edge. With its 18 acres of grounds, central clock tower, accommodation for 200 visitors, a recreation room 40 yards long and a billiard room, it is easy to picture the Victorian or Edwardian seekers of health bickering away their lives in the petty politics of the institution. (Who's been sitting in MY chair?)

Further along the road, there is another imposing building perched on the edge of the hill, the **Queen Victoria School**. However, for me, this is more forbidding than imposing. Perhaps, it is the influence of government, but the main building is grey and plain and cheap-looking, even with its crow-stepped gables.

We now go back into the town, to the **High Street**, a perfectly reasonable assemblage of mainly Victorian buildings with a good mixture of shops at street level and no great evidence yet of the tyranny of the hypermarket.

Turning down, we cross the river and note the **railway station**, where the satisfying little Scottish Baronial core, the writer remembers from his young days is now surrounded by unfortunate modern appendages.

The final stretch of the trail takes us up Springfield Terrace, where the four solid blocks of flats on the left are the **Skye Tenements,** built to house the 19th century millworkers. Around is a humdrum colony of Scottish 2 up, 2 down council houses, giving way to what is almost a new suburb of villas, conveniently close to the A9 and the motorway to Glasgow and Edinburgh.

Chapter Eleven

A Triple Tragedy
Dr Jim Swire and Lockerbie

Still, when I want to learn about a place in Scotland, I first turn to Groome's excellent *Ordnance Gazetteer of Scotland* of 1881, in six volumes. Although, not exactly the last word, it is very strong on the origins of places, and on describing our country in the High Victorian period, when agriculture was still booming, industry was really taking off and towns, large and small, were growing fast.

Lockerbie is on the eastern side of Annandale, the main route from the South to the West of Scotland, followed by the Romans, Thomas Telford, the Caledonian Railway and the A74/M74 in our time. Around a tower-house of the Johnstones of Lockerbie, grew a hamlet, then a village, 'which increased to the bulk of a small provincial town…a neat and thriving place'.

Whatever fame it had come from the lamb fair, the largest in Scotland, when, in August, 50,000 lambs could be snapped up by English dealers for the southern markets.

The railway, 'The Premier Line', played an important role, not always positive. In 1883, 7 people were killed and 25 wounded at Lockerbie station, and in 1928, 4 were killed in a derailment at Dinwoodie, 6 miles north of Lockerbie. But this was nothing compared with the disaster further south at Quintinshill, where 215 of the 1/7th Royal Scots, on their way to Gallipoli, and 11 civilians (4 of them probably children) died in a multiple rail crash and fire.

Towards the end of the 20th century, Lockerbie was drowsing towards that kind of decay all small towns were experiencing. The reconstructed main road took traffic round the town. No-one stopped there. Fast trains passed through, but did not stop. Small shops and tradesmen were frozen out by the big boys.

Nothing remarkable in this, until, at 7.02 pm on 21 December 1988, Pan Am Flight 103 was blown up in mid-air. All on board, 257 passengers and crew, died. To compound the tragedy, the wings of the plane, containing the aircraft's fuel, fell on Sherwood Crescent, a quiet street on the outskirts of Lockerbie. The resultant explosion and fire wiped out all trace of 11 people and sent the name of Lockerbie round the world.

Pan Am Flight 103 was a regular scheduled flight from Frankfurt to Detroit which stopped off at London Heathrow, and was to make another stopover at John F Kennedy, New York. Most of the passengers (188) were Americans going home for Christmas, many of them students at Syracuse University. Dr Jim Swire, whose daughter was killed in the crash and who is one of the few involved who comes out of the catastrophe with credit, noted that the aircraft was only two-thirds full in the week before Christmas—but that families were told that there were no seats to the US that week.

Yet, they were offered seats on Pan Am 103 for 21 December. This is one of many odd things about the Lockerbie affair, but the UK relatives were summoned to the US Embassy in London to be reassured by President Bush's Commission that there was no sinister explanation for this occurrence.

The outrage did not come as a surprise. But where to begin for an explanation? With Colonel Sir Mark Sykes and Francois Georges-Picot who 'drew a line on the sand' (actually a line with a chinagraph pencil on a map of the Middle East) dividing up, between France and Britain, the still undefeated Ottoman Empire?

Or with Iran Air Flight 655 carrying 290 passengers and crew, mostly on pilgrimage to Mecca, which, on 3 July 1988, was shot down over the Persian Gulf by the US Navy cruiser *Vincennes*. The incident took place in Iranian airspace, over Iran's territorial waters in the Persian Gulf, and on the flight's usual flight path. There were no survivors. The official story was that the rising, slow passenger plane was thought to be a fast descending fighter and that ten warning messages had been sent (but all but three were on the wrong wavelength).

A television crew who happened to be on the *Vincennes* sent around the world footage of the ship's exultant crew. The commander, William C Rogers III, was praised, and in 1990, received the Legion of Merit, while the entire crew were awarded the Combat Action Ribbon. Eventually, the truth began to leak out, and in 1996, the United States and Iran reached a settlement at the International Court of Justice.

The United States expressed deep regret at what had happened, but did not accept liability or apologise. They did, however, make an ex gratia payment of $61.8 million to the families.

Understandably, the action caused uproar in the Middle East. There had already been attempted bomb attacks against American civil aircraft, but these were given a new impetus. In October 1988, a Syrian-based Palestinian group were picked up in Germany and revealed several networks and named individuals. Through Interpol, all airlines were alerted to the danger and security was tightened up.

Specific warnings were intercepted or issued. Heathrow staff were alerted on 25 November, and on 5 December, the US Embassy in Helsinki was warned of an imminent attack on a US airliner.

The Lockerbie bombers had intended that the explosion should occur over the Atlantic, where all the evidence would have been lost. Instead, the bomb exploded as the plane was still rising over the Anglo-Scottish border so that the debris fell almost entirely in Scotland, although some came down in Kielder Forest. That an American plane, with mainly American passengers, fell on Scottish soil, meant that all subsequent action would be subject to Scots law.

Dumfries and Galloway Constabulary was the smallest police force on the British mainland and was suddenly faced with coping with the biggest single disaster in our history. Within hours, Chief Constable Boyd realised that he was now faced with solving the biggest crime ever known in our country. Lockerbie and the surrounding area was declared a crime scene, which meant that all 'finds', human or material, had to be meticulously recorded, labelled and stored for analysis.

At 7.33 pm, Channel 4 TV news broadcast the first news of the disaster and Lockerbie became the focus for emergency vehicles, police in unmarked buses and intrusive reporters. There was little need for ambulances, there were no survivors of the crash and only 7 Lockerbie inhabitants had to be taken to Glasgow Royal Infirmary. The next day, the relatives of the deceased began to arrive, although the bodies of their loved ones were still to be recovered.

Bill Hermiston was in charge of the East Lothian Disaster Unit and was telephoned by his chief constable at 10 pm, and instructed to choose 6 sergeants and 30 constables and have them report to Princes Street in Edinburgh at 4 am next morning. They were taken by bus to Lockerbie, where they had no breakfast and found themselves having to search a strange countryside with no maps or radio communication.

After the first day, they had the support of a helicopter manned by trainees from Glencorse Barracks, near Edinburgh, and radio amateurs provided the links between police headquarters and the various parties of searchers out in the fields.

Lockerbie Academy was taken over as police headquarters. (At one point, 2300 were based there. There were to be over 9,250 leads and over 10,000 witnesses). The ice rink was where the bodies and body parts were temporarily accommodated and a disused chemicals factory became the central police warehouse, with a special section for drugs finds.

There was no chance that the investigation was going to be left to the local police. The US government was later to deny that any of its employees had reached the town before around 11 pm—but their suspiciously early arrival makes one wonder if they were expecting something to happen. Soon: 'The countryside around Lockerbie was crawling with unsupervised Americans', clearly searching for 'certain highly sensitive items', and removing debris without authorisation.

And at every stage, the legitimate investigators, even though they were reinforced by outside experts, were subject to procrastination, obfuscation and downright opposition from those who should have wanted the truth brought out into the open.

Some day we may have an honest account of the investigation by one of those closely involved in it. But we can still guess at the experiences of the investigators and the enormous amount of work they put in, in Britain and over a dozen countries abroad; having to cope with other people's legal systems, often operating in a foreign language with every opportunity for misunderstanding and deception.

The first thoughts were that Lockerbie was a straight act of revenge for the *Vincennes* incident. The focus soon shifted on to Syria and Palestine. When the focus shifted to Libya in October 1989, Syria and Palestine were exonerated.

There was, as far as I know, only one 'VIP' on the plane, all the others were little people. Bernt Carlsson was the UN Commissioner for Namibia, who was on the way to New York to attend the signing ceremony giving Namibia independence under the auspices of the United Nations on 22 December—two days after Lockerbie. Namibia remained under the control of apartheid South Africa from 1988 and did not gain full independence until 1990.

Four months after Lockerbie, Mrs Thatcher toured South Africa, taking in the Rossing uranium mine operated (illegally) by Rio Tinto Zinc (British-controlled). This, she declared 'made her proud to be British'. Bernt Carlsson was Lockerbie's highest profile victim, yet the authorities and the media never mention him. Why?

Brilliant forensic work had traced the origin of the bomb to Malta. Flight 103 was really two flights, not one. Flight 103A was a Boeing 727 feeding in to Heathrow from Frankfurt. There the luggage (and passengers) would transfer to the Boeing 747. Amazingly, the detectives were able to identify the suitcase in which the bomb was secreted, its actual place in the hold and the provenance of the timing mechanism. They were also able to trace that the bomb had originated in Malta and had been transferred twice, in Frankfurt and in London.

Unfortunately, the investigation also revealed that the procedures at Frankfurt and London were not as they should have been. The mass of forensic evidence at the trial was presented by the British government's explosives forensic laboratory of the Royal Armament Research and Development Establishment (RARDE), till 1991 at Woolwich.

RARDE's reputation was very high, but very soon became tarnished. In 1991, a convicted IRA bomber successfully appealed when RARDE 'knowingly placed a false and distorted scientific picture before the jury'. In the case of the Maguire Seven, there was a catalogue of failures to disclose evidence and RARDE had to acknowledge that their lab was contaminated with nitro-glycerine.

Danny MacNamee (Hyde Park bombing 1987) was released in 1998, three crucial claims in RARDE's evidence having been dismissed as 'nonsense'. In two cases in 1982 and 1985, two businessmen were convicted on terrorist conspiracy charges. John Berry's appeal was granted in 1993 on the basis of the 'uncompromising and discriminating' evidence of RARDE.

The evidence in Hasan Assali's case was 'open to grave doubt' and the case review may have been delayed deliberately for five years, so as not to compromise the Lockerbie trial.

At the Lockerbie trial, Tony Gauci was one of the prosecution's star witnesses, backed up by his brother, Paul. Tony gave 19 statements to the police and his brother another 4. Gauci was able to identify the accused and describe clothing which had been purchased in his shop in Malta—traces of which had been found in the wreckage.

(The Scottish Criminal Cases Review Commission established that Tony and Paul were paid under the US Government's Rewards for Justice programme, respectively, 2 million and 1 million dollars.)

From the Gauci's evidence and the great mass of forensic evidence, two Libyan intelligence officers, emerged as the prime suspects and in the fullness of time, the case went for trial before Scotland's High Court of Justiciary in the shape of three Scottish judges in the neutral location of Camp Zeist in the Netherlands.

John Ashton and Ian Ferguson commented in vigorous style:

Innocent until proven guilty. It is the most sacred principle of criminal law, but in the Lockerbie case, it was jettisoned from day one. On 14 November 1991, Abdel Basset Ali Al-Megrahi and Lamin Khalifa Fhimah were not only indicted for the bombing, but were also, in effect, tried and convicted. The British and American authorities willingly colluded with the process, letting it be known that they had a cast-iron case—the police had got the right men, end of story.

The US State Department even issued 'fact sheets' outlining the evidence against the two men and the media on both sides of the Atlantic were quietly briefed that Lockerbie was Gaddafi's revenge for America's 1986 air raids on Libya.

Within a few days of the issuing of the indictments, American and British hostages began to be released by Iranian-backed terrorists, Terry Waite being one of the first two.

Not the least irritating feature of the Lockerbie affair is the unconscionable length of time every establishment process seemed to take. On 3 May 2000, eleven years, four months and thirteen days after the murders, the trial opened. It lasted till Wednesday, 31 January 2001, and came up with a surprise result.

The verdicts were greeted with almost universal shock. Among those who had not followed the trial closely, there was shock that one of the accused (Fhimah) had been acquitted. Among many of those who had closely observed proceedings, the shock was that either one could be convicted.

Ashton and Ferguson ruefully point out that the very first sentence of the 82-page judgment contained a glaring error—the judges had got the date of the bombing wrong. They went on to say:

But that howler was nothing compared with what was to follow. Readers who had been shocked by the verdict, were left astounded by the amalgamation of selective evidence and eccentric logic marshalled by the judges in support of their verdict. One of the core principles of criminal justice is that guilt must be proved beyond reasonable doubt. Time and time again…doubt had been cast on the prosecution evidence, yet time and time again the judgment seemed to award the Crown the benefit of those doubts.

Since Megrahi had been found guilty of murder, the judges had to impose a life sentence; Lord Sutherland announcing that he would serve twenty years. On 14 March 2002, an appeal was rejected by 5 judges and the following day, Megrahi was flown to Barlinnie Prison in Glasgow. An interested observer at the trial described the trial and appeal decisions as a 'spectacular miscarriage of justice'.

In 2003, Gaddafi accepted responsibility for the Lockerbie bombing and paid compensation to the families of the victims, although he maintained that he had never given the order for the attack.

Pushed by the SCCRC (and hampered by the Scottish Office), a second appeal began on 28 April 2009 and was soon subject to substantial delays. Meanwhile, Megrahi had been diagnosed with terminal prostate cancer and applied for release on compassionate grounds. On 12 August, he dropped his appeal and was granted compassionate release, to howls of outrage from various parties.

Kenny Macaskill, the Scottish Justice Secretary, was roundly abused for what might have been called Christian compassion towards a dying man.

I clearly remember the news being broken on the Today news programme of the BBC. In America, two parents of victims were interviewed. From their names and accents, they were Jewish and they proceeded to pour out messages of hate and vengeance on both Megrahi and Macaskill. We talk about Judaeo-Christian values as though they are the same, forgetting that they are not. Daniel Cohen, whose daughter Theodora had died in the bombing, said:

I cannot imagine having compassion for a mass murderer and terrorist who killed 270 people, while his wife, Susan, in The Daily Telegraph wrote:

You want to feel sorry for anyone, please feel sorry for me, feel sorry for my poor daughter, her body falling a mile through the air.

Dr Jim Swire, who could have been as vindictive as anyone, wrote:
That decision to use compassionate release is for me one aspect of this dreadful case about which I think Scotland should be proud.

Megrahi had been given three months to live but contrived to stay alive until 20 May 2012—thanks to his more congenial home environment and drugs not available to the NHS. More howls of rage from those who thought they had in some way been cheated of their revenge by his prolonged suffering!

This is a huge subject which has generated millions of words and pages and consumed millions of working hours. The author is just an ordinary chap with no particular expertise in the law and no special forensic skills. But he has lived through the various events of the Lockerbie tragedy; kept up with the news and read a lot of books and newspapers.

There is a smell of rotten fish about the whole affair, and for this reason, he has not chosen to write a balanced account of the affair. He has chosen to quote from such as *Cover-up of Convenience: The Hidden Scandal of Lockerbie, On the Trail of Terror: The Inside Story of the Lockerbie Investigation* and *Scotland's Shame: Why Lockerbie still matters* because he believes they come nearer the truth than officialdom provides. We often learn better from fiction than from supposed fact, and I cannot praise too highly James Robertson's *The Professor of Truth* of 2013.

Robertson formally declares that he 'has drawn on the Lockerbie bombing and conviction of Abdelbaset al-Megrahi as inspiration'. The characters, dialogue, interaction, places...'are either the products of the author's imagination or used in a fictitious manner'.

Part One ('Ice') takes us through the bombing, the investigation, the trial and up to the death of 'Khalil Khasar', through the eyes of Alan Tealing, whose wife and daughter were killed in the bombing. Part Two ('Fire') takes us to Australia and comes to a conclusion which has satisfied many in Britain, but has caused huge antipathy in the US.

Too many countries and too many politicians have been involved for an honest resolution of the problem to be achieved. We would like to think that we live in a country—whether Scotland or Britain—where the establishment ensures that justice reigns and the little man (or woman) is protected. But a Scotsman in London, carrying a table leg, is shot dead by a policeman in the belief that he is an Irishman carrying a rifle. The policeman is exonerated from any wrongdoing.

A young, unarmed Brazilian is pursued through the streets into an underground station and on to a train where, lying prone and defenceless on the floor, he is despatched with 7 shots to the head. Again, the police involved were exonerated from any wrongdoing and, indeed, the superordinate officer in charge of the whole operation was gradually promoted till she reached the summit of the greasy pole—Chief Constable of the Metropolitan Police.

Willie MacRae was an SNP activist and anti-nuclear campaigner. On 6 April 1985, he was found in his car about 90 feet from the A87 west of Glenmoriston. He was still alive and breathing and was taken to hospital in Inverness, then to Aberdeen Royal Infirmary, where a nurse discovered a wound in his head. An X-ray detected a bullet in his head.

His brain was severely damaged, and on 7 April, his life-support machine was switched off. Next day, a revolver without fingerprints was found 60 feet from the car. MacRae carried with him everywhere two cases of confidential documents because his house had been burgled so many times. These had disappeared.

MacRae's death was ruled to be suicide. There has been no Fatal Accident Inquiry and no medical reports or post-mortem data have been released to the public.

Activists, a Channel 4 broadcast, an STV episode and two plays have come 'up against a brick wall' in their search for the truth, but there were signs that resistance might be beginning to crumble. Late in 2014, an alleged paedophile ring in Westminster in the 1980s went viral and the *Scottish Sunday Express* suggested that the contents of the missing briefcases might have been connected with this.

A crusading journalist asked Police Scotland six factual questions, which they declined to answer. On 30 June 2015, the Freedom of Information Commissioner ruled that Police Scotland withheld information from journalist Paul Delamore.

If police fail to release this information, the Court of Session may place them in contempt of court.

A small victory, perhaps, but a victory. Even more interesting were some of the Commissioner's comments.

The commissioner notes that there has been a significant level of public distrust regarding the original investigation into the death of Mr MacRae. She takes the view that disclosure of additional factual information about the case could be in the public interest, by helping to establish the known facts and, in doing so, perhaps help dispel public distrust.

But, once again, the issue was allowed to run into the sand.

On the 30th anniversary of MacRae's death, a petition for a Fatal Accident Inquiry into the case was to be presented to the Lord Advocate, Frank Mulholland QC. The petitioners reported as follows:

Lord Advocate told the media (two days before we even handed your signatures into his office) he would not approve a Fatal Accident Inquiry for Willie McRae. Also we are now two months after the hand in and he still hasn't even responded to your petition directly, in my opinion this shows not only arrogance but a high degree of disrespect to the 12,000+ signers.

An excellent example of what is known in the trade as 'kicking into the long grass'.

Right at the end of 2014, the Lord Advocate was to the fore in a 2-page spread in *Scotland on Sunday*. His headline was:

Scotland's top law officer: Megrahi WAS guilty of Lockerbie atrocity.

Lord Advocate says inquiry will focus on tracking down 'accomplices'.

And beside it, John Ashton, author of two of the books above, wrote:

The four elephants in the room which suggest the Lord Advocate is wrong…

The Scottish Criminal Cases Review Commission came as close as it legally could to saying that the guilty verdict was itself wrong.

It would have been nice to think that we were on the brink of something big, and that the relatives of those who died at Lockerbie might find some resolution to their anxieties, but again—to change the metaphor—the quest for truth ran into the sand.

The smell of fish refuses to disperse. Released Cabinet papers recently divulged that: 'Lockerbie public inquiry was ruled out within hours', and that the Prime Minister Margaret Thatcher, the day after the outrage, said:

It was not clear that that any further public inquiry would be required in addition to the local procurator fiscal's inquiry, and no commitments about such a further inquiry should therefore be made.

It beggars belief that a prime minister should have been advised to make such a categorical statement almost before the fumes from the catastrophe had dispersed.

Dr Jim Swire, father of a victim and the leading campaigner for justice, commented that:

One of the things this indicates is the entrenched view among ministers that they should limit the public's access to the truth about what happened.

This was not a matter for party politics. In 2009, the then Prime Minister, Gordon Brown, also ruled out a public inquiry.

It may be instructive to look at the two massive disasters which intruded into the peace of Dumfriesshire. Quintinshill was terrible, with an initial crash compounded by a second collision and fire. But it was clean in the sense that it was a genuine accident, the straightforward consequence of stupidity, poor management, carelessness and inattention. It could be said to be a family affair, kept quiet because it occurred in wartime.

The men responsible were arrested, tried and imprisoned. Sentence served, they were re-employed by the Caledonian Railway. (Revisionists say they carried the can for the company, which went unpunished for providing unsatisfactory rolling stock and for failing to supervise the signalmen properly).

Lockerbie was quite different. It was a deliberate, planned mass murder, the only miscalculation being that the explosion occurred over land and earlier than planned. It was an episode in an international game of tit-for-tat, with no beginning and no end in sight, and in which the pieces are of no account to the big players. And the big players were and are the biggest.

Lockerbie was the site of multiple tragedies. There were the deaths, of people returning home for Christmas and of talented young people about to contribute to society. Then there was the tragedy of those at home, knowing and not knowing, and their churlish treatment by officialdom. Then there was the tragedy of those who rated national interests and position higher than human understanding and compassion.

And throughout runs the uncomfortable feeling that a scapegoat was punished while the guilty have gone free, and are probably chortling away quietly in comfortable retirement.

In May 2015, Kenny MacAskill, by then out of office and free to speak his mind, came out with *The Lockerbie Bombing: The Search for Justice*. At the Edinburgh International Book Festival in 2016, he was reported as having said: 'We were stitched up over bomber release' and 'Scotland set up over Lockerbie bomber release'.

It seemed as if MacAskill was trying to disassociate himself—and indeed the Scottish legal system—from the murky details of the incident and its consequences. In effect, he is saying: 'a big boy threw a stone and ran away'.

James Robertson, author and member of Justice for Megrahi, reviewed the book and was not impressed. 'Where is the justice?' The headline screamed. Robertson, besides questioning MacAskill's journalistic and forensic competence, wondered why 'if he does have information pertinent to the case, he should share it with Police Scotland'. Robertson's conclusion is that:

The Lockerbie case has long been a stain on the Scottish justice system. Kenny rubs and rubs at that stain. Whatever his intent, the effect is not to make it vanish but to make it look far worse.

Not many members of the Establishment come out of this situation well. One, Douglas Hurd, British Foreign Secretary, did recognise that Dr Jim Swire was a 'sensible man with whom it is important to keep in touch', realising that Dr Swire's daughter, Flora, was one of those killed. Unfortunately, the Establishment chose to ignore this advice and Dr Swire was forced into the role of gadfly.

Dr Swire was a GP of Scots descent in Worcestershire. He had spent much of his youth in Scotland. His wife was Scottish and they have a second home in Skye, which was especially loved by their daughter.

After Lockerbie, Dr Swire said that:

There was no support group, no protocol and many mistakes were made. We were kept in the dark by the authorities and treated insensitively by politicians and the media. It took many years of persistence to feel we had achieved any level of justice.

In Britain, most of the families coalesced into a UKFamiliesFlight103 (UKFF103) group, for which Dr Swire became spokesman, although never formally elected.

To demonstrate the incompetence and inflexibility of the aircraft security system, he took a fake bomb, made of a radio cassette player and marzipan, on a flight from Heathrow to New York and from there to Boston. Professor Black of Edinburgh University and he contrived to have Megrahi put on trial in a Scots court in the Netherlands in 2000—a mere eleven years after the outrage! As we saw earlier, the outcome was that Megrahi was found guilty—'Swire fainted and had to be carried from the courtroom'.

Swire visited Megrahi in jail (and later in Libya) and founded the Justice for Megrahi Campaign. Swire lobbied in Britain, America, the United Nations, Germany and Libya. Once Megrahi had been released, Dr Swire visited him in Libya.

Many American families of victims criticised Swire for his supposed support for Libya, while Lord Fraser of Carmyllie, the former Lord Advocate, suggested that Swire was suffering from 'Stockholm syndrome', in which captives grow to admire and defend their captors. And there were the usual hate mail and death threats.

Dr Swire was adept at using recent releases of selected government papers under the 30-year rule to raise 'dire questions about the function of the Scottish criminal prosecution authorities' and to question:

where the prosecution...chooses to sequester many of those facts from the eyes of the defence and the court.

Every now and then, Dr Swire dashed off an authoritative letter to the press anent Lockerbie and security. When a memory stick with 76 unencrypted files relating to core aspects of Heathrow's security was found in a London street, he launched into an attack on the complacency and inaction of the authorities, repeating the gross blunders made with respect of Pan Am 103.

No search was made, nor were any flights cancelled. If such precautions had been taken, my daughter and 269 others might still be alive today.

But one can picture the great ones of this world, if they could even be bothered reading Swire's letter, grunting and mouthing—'Oh no! Not him again!'

His struggles with authority have not been without cost. Dr Swire's medical partners sacked him because he was spending too much time away from his GP duties. He lost part of his pension and money was tight. The Swires had to downsize from their roomy country home with 17 acres of land, though they have kept the wood they planted in Flora's memory. He says, he:

Had to do locums and I was taken on as an assistant by my old practice, which took a certain amount of, suppression of feelings shall we say, on my part.

We all admire David, the little chap who took on the big bully with a scrap of leather and a handful of stones from the burn. How much more does Dr Swire impress us with his heroic stance against at least three Goliaths, in the face of mighty prejudice and self-interest? A Great Scot indeed!

Nevertheless, it does seem, from time to time, that the climate is changing. Despite the obfuscation of the great ones kicking the issue into the long grass, there is, in many quarters, a quiet acceptance of the innocence of Megrahi and a realisation that the main culprit is still alive somewhere in the Middle East.

Not unrelated to the Lockerbie/Libya question was a recent public apology in parliament by the prime minister (and award of £500,000 in compensation) to two Gaddafi dissidents (one heavily pregnant) who had been arrested in Thailand in 2004, 'redacted and tortured by the CIA with the compliance of the British Government'. Murky waters indeed!

Yet recently, there has been another setback, when Megrahi's relatives sought to have his case reconsidered but, yet again, hidden forces saw to it that their pleas were ignored.

At the same time, late in 2022, a case was brought against an individual who was supposed to be one of the makers of the Lockerbie bomb. How successful this will be is anyone's guess, one of the complications being that the disaster occurred over Scottish soil and therefore must be dealt with under Scots law.

I have chosen to name this chapter a triple tragedy. There was the diabolical atrocity of destroying the lives of people returning home for Christmas, of talented young people soon to contribute to society and of innocents asleep in their beds in the town. There was the tragedy of those at home, bereft, knowing and not knowing, and their churlish treatment by officialdom.

Then there was perhaps the greatest tragedy of all; the tragedy of those who rated national interests and personal position higher than human understanding and compassion, and truth.

'Closure' is the fashionable word these days, but after thirty years, for the friends and relatives of the victims who are still alive, there is still no closure and little prospect of any. The establishment must have something very unsavoury indeed to conceal.

Burns, as usual, had words for the situation:

> Man's inhumanity to Man
> Makes countless thousands mourn!

The Trail

Is a Lockerbie Trail just an example of the modern trend of 'disaster tourism'? Should there be anything so crass as a trail for such a tragic affair? Or am I just pandering to voyeurism? Encouraging empty-headed tourists to take 'selfies' in front of the scars of tragedy?

On the edge of many Mediterranean towns, there is a chapel on a hill, with a pedestrian way leading up to it, often bordered by junipers or cypresses. This is the Via Crucis or Via Dolorosa. On the way up are the Stations of the Cross, recording the stages on Christ's last journey, from his condemnation to death to his being laid in the tomb. At each station, the pilgrim will halt to pray, to meditate or merely to catch his breath or admire the view.

This Lockerbie Trail is offered in the same kind of spirit, not as a form of sightseeing but as a structure on which the serious visitor can build his or her own reflections.

1. **Tundergarth Kirk** is on the B7068, about 3 miles east of Lockerbie. For the purpose of the trail, it is best approached from Langholm. The church itself is big and massive and not particularly old, but in the kirkyard is a little watch house built in the 1800s, when the likes of Burke and Hare were on the hunt for bodies for medical students to practise on. This has been converted for visitors to see personal memorials and record their feelings.

The field across the road was the most accessible of the disaster sites. Here the biggest piece of debris, the nose cone of the plane, landed, very conveniently for photographers.

From here into Lockerbie, it is easy to imagine how frustrating the efforts of the searchers for survivors and evidence must have been. There is scarcely any flat land. There are little hills and little valleys, hedges and copses, a river in a gorge and, getting nearer to Lockerbie, plantations of trees. (At Kielder, further east, fragments of plane and people were found thirty feet up in the trees).

Imagine the stress and horror of the police and volunteers as they struggled across this scene of devastation in the foul weather of short, dark December days.

2. **Sherwood Crescent.** Proceed down into Lockerbie, over the railway to the centre, where there are a few quite handsome buildings. In Lockerbie Town Hall Council Chambers, there is a suitable stained-glass window. Up to the right is the Dryfesdale Parish Church, with a memorial and a book of remembrance.

    Turning down to the left, we follow the old A74 as the town becomes shabbier, with the usual disused cinema. Just before we leave the town, we turn right at a garage and find ourselves in a pleasant little area of winding roads, bungalows and little villas.

There is a big gap in Sherwood Crescent, filled with a modest garden of grass and big evergreens. This is where the wing section of the plane crashed, exploded and went on fire, totally consuming the houses and their residents.

The author clearly remembers May 1989, when he was driving south on the A74 past the disaster site and shuddered to see the huge hollow made by the plane.

The garden is quite unpretentious, its impact comes from the contrast between the neatness of suburbia broken by the sombre green of the big shrubs. Almost like a maze, there is in the garden a small monument.

3. Dryfesdale Lodge Visitor Centre and Garden of Remembrance.

Turn back towards the town centre, and at the first set of traffic lights, turn left along the A709. After about a mile is the town cemetery. The first thing one comes to is a block of five cherry trees, each dedicated to a named victim. A neat sandstone gatekeeper's lodge has been turned into the Dryfesdale Lodge Visitor Centre. It has photographs and a display, a book of remembrance and an area for reflection and reassurance.

Beyond the unremarkable sections for the good folk of Lockerbie and district, we come to the Garden of Remembrance, unfussy and almost formal. There is a double avenue of cherries, each with its named subject. There is a ring of cypresses. Then there is a formal layout in front of the boundary wall of the cemetery. The Air Disaster Memorial (PLATE 8b) has the names of all the victims, and there is a miscellany of individual tablets and stones put there by the families.

A decent attempt has been made to smooth over the terrible destruction of 21 December 1988. Many visitors come here for whatever purpose. Let us hope that, despite all the unanswered questions, they can derive some comfort and peace of mind in these surroundings.

Chapter Twelve

A Bewitching Place
The Astronomer Royal and Schiehallion

The Reverend Nevil Maskelyne FRS (1732-1811) is not a name to conjure with in the 21st century, but he has his claim to greatness. Living at a time when Britons were venturing vast distances across all the world's oceans, he played his part in enabling seamen to find out exactly where they were on these trackless seas.

Born in London, educated at Cambridge and with a living in Northamptonshire, his vision was directed south rather than to the north— although John Playfair, Hutton's companion on the Siccar Point excursion, proposed him for the Royal Society of Edinburgh.

As an astronomer, Maskelyne was heavily involved in expeditions observing Venus, measuring the distance to the sun and finding a method of determining longitude, vital information for navigators. Dava Sobel's *Longitude: The True Story of a Lone Genius Who Solved the Greatest Scientific Problem of His Time* of 1995, describes in meticulous detail the quest for the exact knowledge of longitude and Maskelyne's part in it.

He made observations from St Helena and Barbados and reported to the Board of Longitude in 1765. Seventeen days later, he was appointed Astronomer Royal, the fifth, a post he was to fill for forty-six years, till his death.

He was now *ex officio* Commissioner of Longitude and supervised the resolution of the longitude question. John Harrison had designed a series of increasingly accurate chronometers (now impressively displayed in the National Maritime Museum at Greenwich). These showed local time along with the time at Greenwich.

The time difference between the two places was a measure of longitude. (24 hours = 360 degrees, therefore, for example, a difference of four minutes means one degree of longitude.)

Harrison now received a reward of £10,000 under the 1714 Longitude Act. A further £10,000 would be awarded if he could demonstrate the replicability and accuracy of his chronometer. This he duly collected! The size of the award and the time taken to earn it show how important this development was for a maritime nation like ours.

Maskelyne's solution, based on astronomical observations of the lunar-distance of the moon, was not submitted to the Board for reward, but was adopted as a check on the timekeeper on a long voyage. *The British Mariner's Guide* embodied the procedures and tables for finding longitude at sea.

After longitude, Maskelyne involved himself in the precise measurement of a degree of latitude. He co-operated with Count Cassini in Paris, who headed up the first national survey, the first sheet of which was published in 1756. Britain followed with the Ordnance Survey, headed by General Roy, whose work began in earnest in 1790.

Astronomical work involved observations of Venus, tides at St Helena and Barbados. Maskelyne is credited with the introduction of measurement of time to tenths of a second.

The French, innovative as ever, in the guise of Pierre Bouguer and Charles-Marie de la Condamine, had devised an experiment in 1738 for the establishment of the Earth's density, and hence its weight. They carried it out on Chimborazo, a volcano in what is now Ecuador, but were not satisfied with the results. In 1772, Maskelyne, fresh from observations made during the survey of the Mason-Dixon Line in Maryland and Pennsylvania, turned his attention to weighing the Earth.

He suggested that the weight of the earth could be calculated by the deflection of a pendulum by the pull of a mountain of known weight. We all know that, if an apple becomes detached from a branch of the tree, it falls to the ground. The mass of the earth attracts the mass of the apple and pulls it down. And we know and can calculate the speed with which the apple falls, the time it takes and its terminal velocity.

In 1950, the author passed Higher Dynamics in the Scottish Leaving Certificate, having demonstrated that he knew how to make such calculations, as well as measuring the impact of cannonballs and the effect of a 15-degree slope on the speed of a train.

Less obvious is that the mass of the apple exerts a pull on the earth and pulls it up by an almost untraceable amount. Calculation of this would seem to be beyond the wit of man. But not beyond the wit of he who concerned himself with measuring the weight of the earth. All that was necessary was to find a suitable mountain, of a shape easily measured, of uniform composition so that its weight could be calculated and far enough away from other mountains to be unaffected by their pull.

The Royal Society set up a Committee of Attraction, with Maskelyne as a member, and despatched the astronomer and surveyor Charles Mason to find such a mountain. Over the summer of 1773 Mason searched, concluding that the best candidate would be the quartzite Schiehallion. Mason declined to carry out the experiment for a commission of one guinea per day, so it fell to Maskelyne to get temporary leave from his duties as Astronomer Royal, in order to manage the experiment.

This was real pioneering work and it took till 1776 to complete the task. The surveyors had to start from scratch. Because Schiehallion is an east-west ridge, the slopes north and south are very steep, so that measurements could be made close to the mountain's core. The first task was to build two observatories, one on either side of the mountain, a stone bothy and a tented encampment.

Thus the deflection of a pendulum could be measured on the north side, then on the south side. The mean of the two readings would give a measure of Schiehallion's pull. There were no maps so a detailed basic survey had to be made, often in the worst of Highland weather, using theodolites and chains backed and checked by astronomical observations. In the course of operations, Charles Hutton, Maskelyne's right-hand man, 'discovered' what we now call contours as a means of showing relief from a mass of isolated measured heights.

Laborious and crude the work may have been, but it came up with a very reasonable result. Maskelyne's calculations gave a value for the density of the Earth with an error of less than 20%, and several subsequent investigations have refined, but not contradicted, the work of Maskelyne and Hutton.

They also discovered that the surface rocks were less dense than the core of the Earth, and surmised that the core material might be metallic and might be 65% of the core. We now call it NiFe (= NickelFe/Iron).

Now, this is all very well, Maskelyne was clearly a Great Man, but a Great Scot? My answer is that anyone who spends four years of his working life on and around a Scottish mountain, in fair weather and foul, must have become a Scot by residence and special registration!

Schiehallion! Schiehallion! Schiehallion! What a splendid name! It rings around like a trumpet blast! And what a splendid mountain Schiehallion is!

Between the Tay and Tummel valleys in Highland Perthshire, its east-west ridge stands apart from the other big hills. From the A9, north of Blair Atholl, its peak peeps over low hills; although woodland growth makes this a chancy business for the driver.

The view from Loch Rannoch is one of the most photographed in Scotland. Through the birches around the loch, the opposite shores rise up to a perfect cone, snow-clad in winter, which has graced many a calendar, postcard or exhibition entry. Coming south on the West Highland Line across the scraped and tortured Moor of Rannoch, one can often see this fairy hill 20 miles (30Km) off, glowing in the sun's setting rays.

As a mountain, Schiehallion is sizeable rather than formidable. At 1083 metres (3547 feet), it ranks as number 66 in Munro's Tables. (For comparison, Snowdon, the highest summit 'furth of Scotland', is 2 metres higher than Schiehallion). But Schiehallion's reputation does not depend on its height, but on its character.

'The hills are alive'. To the end of 1948, only 13 men and one woman had 'completed' all the Munros. Of these 10 were members of the Scottish Mountaineering Club, a select and experienced group for whom membership is still by invitation only. By 2017, the list of completers had grown to 6179 (the author's number is 453), and they are still regarded with a degree of suspicion by the wee hard men, and women.

With a certain frivolity, Douglas Fraser in *The Lost Leader* (with apologies to the shade of Browning and to at least 73 others) conveys this suspicion of the humble toilers.

> Just for a handful of summits he left us,
> Just for a 'Dearg' to tick on his list.
> Thus Munro's Tables have slowly bereft us,
> Changed Ultramontane to Salvationist.
> Raeburn was with us, Collie was of us.
> Ling, Glover were for us—they watch from belays.
> He alone breaks from the van and the freemen,
> Climbs up his mountains the easiest ways.
> We shall climb prospering—not thro' his presence,
> Leads will inspirit us—not on his rope.
> Deeds will be done while he boasts his collection,

Ben Vane to Braeriach, Mount Keen to Ben Hope.
Blot out his name then, record one lost soul more,
One more peak-bagger to collect them all.
Pelt him with pitons and crown him with crampons,
Leave him spread-eagled on Rubicon Wall!

Seton Gordon (1886-1977), naturalist, photographer, folklorist, writer and Highland gentleman, was particularly fond of Schiehallion. In his *Highways and Byways in the Central Highlands* of 1935, he did what so few can do for the Highlands, successfully balancing scientific observation, appreciation of landscape and the supernatural.

Seton Gordon does not gush about the beauty of Schiehallion in extended descriptions. Instead, as he goes around interpreting the landscape, the mountain comes in as a backdrop—'the fairy hill of the Caledonians veils herself in sorrow', 'away to the west rose Schiehallion, a cloud fired by the setting sun resting on its picturesque summit', in late September 'a thin cap of mist clothed the summit...and as the mist rose and fell, it showed at times a faint golden gleam as the sun lit up the fringes of the cloud'.

From Ben Alder, 25Km to the north-west, Seton Gordon was able to see, in June—'above Schiehallion's cone white shafts of hail were descending earthward'.

In Highland Perthshire, there are still some odd survivals of the past. On the low ground are many standing stones from Neolithic times and the Bronze Age, often supervised by Iron Age forts. In a lonely side-glen above (the reservoir) Loch na Daimh in upper Glen Lyon, the shepherd every spring brings out from their little house a stone family of father, mother and children and sets them out on a platform in the sun, to be returned to their house as winter approaches.

In the lovely little church at Innerwick in Glen Lyon, there is an old bell, dating from the old Celtic church. Seton Gordon mentions 5 others in this area in his time and there were others further west. The oldest date from the 8th century and are associated with St Columba, Iona and the missions to the Picts. These early bells were rectangular and made of an iron sheet, folded and riveted. The 9th century bells were cast in bronze. Although, they may look primitive... three of these exhibit a characteristic, unique to their design, of producing three distinct notes of different pitch from three of the four faces.

Such special objects necessitated special care and custodianship of the bell was an honour and became hereditary. In the case of the Dewars, this hereditary responsibility lasted until the 19th century. The name 'Dewar' derives from *deoradh*, which relates to travel, as the bell was a holy relic, to be taken around the countryside.

As one would expect, these Celtic bells had remarkable properties and were often stolen. St Adamnan's bell (St Adamnan was Columba's biographer and ninth abbot of Iona) from Insh in Invernessshire was stolen and taken off south. As the rascals were going over the Pass of Drumochter, the bell refused to keep silent and rang out indignantly its name—'Tom Eonan! Tom Eunon!'

Seton Gordon very gently suggests a similarity between the music of Adamnan's bell and the cries of the whooper swans which each year fly south-east from Iceland to winter upon the waters of Loch Insh!

St Fillan's bell, a cast bronze bell, was placed over a sufferer's head during healing rituals in order to heal such afflictions as migraine headaches. Legend has it that the bell would come to St Fillan when called. It seems to have been stolen quite frequently but had the disconcerting habit of flying back to its home overnight!

One day, a visitor who was unused to seeing bells flying through the air was startled and shot it with an arrow, causing a crack which is still there.

However, on 9 August 1798, it was impudently stolen by an English tourist, who recorded the episode in his diary:

In order to ascertain the truth of St Fillan's Bell, I carried it off with me to England. An old woman who saw what I was about, asked me what I wanted with the bell, and I told her I had an unfortunate relation at home out of his mind, and that I wanted to have him cured. 'Oh but,' she says, 'you must bring him here to be cured, or it will be of no use.' Upon which I told her he was too ill to be moved, and off I galloped with the Bell to Tyndrum Inn.

The stolen bell did not fly back to Strathfillan, but was eventually tracked down by Bishop Forbes of the Episcopalian Diocese of Brechin, in 1869. For safe keeping, he had this very special object placed in, what is now, the Scottish National Museum in Edinburgh. It is displayed along with St Fillan's Crozier and Coigreach (the highly-ornamented case for the crozier) in the Kingdom of the Scots gallery of the National Museum of Scotland in Edinburgh.

The fairies of the Celtic fringe were not sweet and lovely like the Sugar Plum Fairy in Tchaikowsky's *Nutcracker*, or Noel Paton's pictures. Rather, they bore more resemblance to the dark figures immortalised by the Brothers Grimm. According to Isobel Grant in *Highland Folk Ways*:

In the past there was a strong element of fear in people's lives. The fairies of the Highlands, politely spoken of as the *Daoine Sith* (Men of Peace), sometimes said to be fallen angels, were generally inimical to the human race. Among their malpractices were the carrying off of new-born babies and replacing them with changelings, and shooting cattle with elf-bolts. No good came of dealing with them.

And they turned the milk sour!

Patrick Geddes wrote of the faerie folk of Celtic legend with great seriousness, and approval!

There pass before us the Riders of the Sidhe, each offering one of the four gifts of life to men. First the leafing, flowering fruiting branch of the Life-Tree—the simple life and labour of the People. The next bears the cup—for the joy of life in its prosperity. The next is gazing into his magic crystal, of Thought; in which, from reflections from without, again from memories within, Emotion, Reason and Intuition are ever creating new visions. Finally, comes the bearer of the Sword—for Idealism in Action, Justice in Rule.

This vision was turned into an intriguing work of Celtic Revival symbolist art by John Duncan in 1911, and is now part of the art collection of the city of Dundee.

Place names demonstrate that the fairies were active all over the Highlands. The last phase of the melting ice resulted in large numbers of little hills and mounds on the lower ground. These little hills—*Tom* in the Gaelic—are often quite distinctive because of their composition of well-drained sands and gravels, which makes them greener than the moorland around.

Examples are, the Inverness cemetery—*Tomnahurich* (hillock the shape of a boat, a coracle), *Tomintoul* (hill like a barn), *Tomnavoulin* (hill of the mill). Few skiers on the way to the ski slopes realise that Glen Shee is the Glen of the Fairies. (The screech of the *banshee*, white fairy, is well-known to readers of Irish fiction). Tomich is *Tomach* (the place of knolls).

Just south of Aberfoyle, the Ordnance Survey show two hills, Doon Hill and Fairy Knowe (knoll in Scots). The former is a perfect cone about 50 metres high while the latter is about the same height but more of a ridge. They are now heavily forested so defy close examination. We will return to the Rev Robert

Kirk, minister of Aberfoyle, seventh son of another Rev Robert Kirk, minister of Aberfoyle in a few moments.

All I would say at this stage, is that Doon Hill is, in my opinion, the fairies hill and it may be that inside it, the good minister may still be whooping it up with the Queen of the Fairies.

Within a mile of the churches of Balquhidder, the OS map shows a feast of antiquities. There is a Rob Roy standing stone and two groups of cup-marked rocks. In the present church is *Clach Aonghuis* (Angus's stone) with an ecclesiastic, holding a cup. In the graveyard, the engraved stone that is labelled 'Rob Roy's grave' is clearly much older than the ambiguous hero, as is proved by the Celtic tracery.

Balquidder has two bells, the less ancient of which was presented to the church by Robert Kirk (c1641-92) in 1685 when he left Balquhidder to take up the charge of Aberfoyle. Kirk certainly lived in challenging times and had an interesting life. In the religious turmoil of the 17th century, he was at first an Episcopalian priest and then converted to become a Presbyterian minister. He bridged two cultures by supervising, in London, the production of a Gaelic Bible. He also translated the metrical psalms into Gaelic.

His unique contribution was not, however, narrowly religious. By about 1691, he had collected and compiled a great deal of material on the supernatural, but died before it could be published. Walter Scott, in 1815, contrived to have it published under the snappy title of *The Secret Commonwealth or an Essay on the Nature and Actions of the Subterranean (and for the most part) Invisible People heretofore going under the names of Fauns and Fairies, or the like, among the Low Country Scots as described by those who have second sight, 1691.*

The Secret Commonwealth, as it is usually known, is still regarded in folkloric circles as one of the most important and authoritative works on fairy folk beliefs.

Scott had a good track record in these matters. Although, he and Goethe never met, they corresponded and respected each other. As Scott rather naively and modestly wrote: 'Goethe is different and a wonderful fellow'. Scott translated Schiller's *The Robbers* in 1799.

In 1802, his *Minstrelsy of the Scottish Border* (which failed to disentangle fact from fiction in respect of Thomas of Ercildoune—c1210-c1290—best-known as 'Thomas the Rhymer', who was a man of magic and spent seven years in Elfland) went viral in Europe, to be discovered by Achin von Arnim who, with Clemens Brentano, 'practically founded the German Romantic delight in the Rhein', collecting and then publishing folk songs under the title *Des Knaben Wunderhorn*, which was in turn mined successfully by the composer Gustav Mahler.

In 1812-1815, the *Kinder* and *Hausmärchen*—Children and Household, definitely not fairy tales—of the Brothers Grimm were appearing. And at the same time as the collectors were picking the brains of the peasants ETA, Hoffmann's strange imagination provided the spark for a dozen operas, ballets and the novel of suspense, including *The Nutcracker and the Mouse King* in 1815 (Favourite Christmas ballet—*The Nutcracker*).

His Dr Coppelius is the amusingly eccentric creator of a living doll in the Delibes ballet *Coppelia* and the evil opponent of Hoffmann in Offenbach's *Tales of Hoffmann*, who four times in an evening does Hoffmann down and goes off with the girl.

The Brocken, in the Harz Mountains, is exactly the same height as Lochnagar in Deeside, and there is nothing of equal height between them. Goethe climbed the Brocken in February and found it damp, dark and miserable. The Brocken Spectre, first described in 1780, adds to the mystery of an area already well-known for witches and unholy ongoings.

When it came to writing his greatest work, *Faust*, Goethe chose the Brocken as the place where Faust sold his soul to the Devil, prompting some of Berlioz's most terrifying music in *The Damnation of Faust.*

Walt Disney carried on these traditions. Snow White is straight out of Grimm, as is her wicked stepmother. The Seven Dwarves toiled in the silver mines of the Harz, only recently closed after a thousand years of operations. All over the mountains are dams and lades, leading the water down to operate the processing machinery.

With a good view of Schiehallion, in Glen Fincastle north of the Tummel, are two interesting sites. A wooded knoll south-west of the Mains of Fincastle, is named *An Sithean*, the Fairy Hill. West of this is Edintain, which is, according to Seton Gordon, *Aodann an t-Sithein,* Face of the Fairy Hill.

One of the problems of the name Schiehallion is that 'the fairy hill of the Caledonians' is like no other fairy hill. It is huge, rocky and well away from settled or cultivated land—quite unlike any of the other fairy hills.

A likely explanation—which suits me—is that *Aodann an t-Sithein* faces on to Schiehallion (as well as its neighbouring Fairy Hill) and recognises the great mountain as a kind of capital of the fairy hills—bigger, just as shapely, but more powerful. A kind of symbol of the power of the fairies.

So we have Schiehallion the beautiful, Schiehallion the mystical, Schiehallion the key to knowledge about the Earth. What about Schiehallion and the Romantics? Nothing much about the fairies, is there something bigger? The Romantics may have revelled in Nature, but, as Byron wrote: 'England, thy beauties are tame and domestic'.

Wordsworth was most comfortable with his daffodils, the little celandine, the border rivers and his 'sweet Highland girl'. Housman *On Wenlock Edge* (1083 feet) is nostalgic, not sublime.

Yet Coleridge, opium-soaked creator of *The Rime of the Ancient Mariner*, had his vigorous moments, at the age of 30 making the first recorded descent of Broad Stand between Scafell and Scafell Pike in the Lake District ('Difficult'). In Scotland in 1803, he broke away from the Wordsworths and covered 263 miles in eight days. Although, he made a detour up Glen Nevis, he kept to the recently constructed military roads.

We usually think of John Keats as a true Romantic, gifted but weedy, dying of tuberculosis at the age of 25. Yet he and his friend, Charles Brown, made a pedestrian tour of the Highlands in 1818, in the course of which he/they climbed Ben Nevis, then known as a big mountain but not yet recognised as the highest in the British Isles.

In his sonnet *Written upon the Top of Ben Nevis,* he describes a depressing, sullen, misty, vague landscape and compares it with the human condition faced with mist and crag in the world of thought and mental might.

Read me a lesson, Muse, and speak it loud
    Upon the top of Nevis, blind in mist!
I look into the chasms, and a shroud
    Vapourous doth hide them—just so much I wist
Mankind do know of hell; I look o'erhead
    And there is sullen mist—even so much
Mankind can tell of heaven; mist is spread
    Before the earth, beneath me—even such,
Even so vague is man's sight of himself!

>   Here are the craggy stones beneath my feet
> Thus much I know that, a poor witless elf,
>   I tread on them—that all my eye doth meet
> Is mist and crag, not only on this height,
>   But in the world of thought and mental might.

For Keats, there was no escape to the hills!

Helen B Cruickshank (1886-1975) was one of the Northeast poets who helped to keep their 'speak' alive in a homogenising world. Her Schiehallion is in standard English and is quite long. Here, I quote the first and last stanzas.

> Years, long years ago I read of a death I envied.
> A girl climbing alone on this noble mountain
> With its glittering quartzite cone,
> Was caught by a thunderstorm,
> Struck by lightning,
> And killed.
>
> I think of the hills in their pure clear air
> And that man-made clouds of poison
> May rest upon them, and us,
> Annihilating all;
> And I long to reach the crest
> Of my earthly life and gain
> Schiehallion.

Cruickshank clearly had a multi-facetted view of Schiehallion, as a fact of nature, subject to all its forces, as an escape from the sordid realities of modern life, an escape polluted by the multiplication of these realities. For her, Schiehallion was also a metaphor for life itself, a kind of pilgrim's progress to a better life.

Edwin Morgan (1920-2010) was the last survivor of the so-called 'Big Seven' of the Scottish Renaissance. During World War 2, he served as a non-combatant conscientious objector with the Royal Army Medical Corps. He loved playing with words, mastered all the poetic forms and translated from at least nine languages.

In his will, he left £918,000 to the Scottish National Party, and another £1 million for the creation of an annual award scheme for young poets in Scotland.

One of his wittiest poems is CANEDOLIA—an off-concrete scotch fantasia. (Note to the typesetter—this is not a typo, this is the title). This is a marvellous evocation of Scottish place-names. After the introduction (oa! hoy! awe! ba! mey!), the format is of a series of questions, each being answered by a list of onomatopoeic answers, often rhyming. For example:

what is it like to be there?

Och it's freuchie, it's faifley, it's wamphray, it's frandy, it's sliddery.

'But who was there?' invites a long answer, which in turn invites the question: 'and what was the toast?'

The answer sums up the Scot's pride and exaltation:

Schiehallion! Schiehallion! Schiehallion!

The Trail

Hill people don't need a trail which goes something like this: Drive to car park at Grid Reference so-and-so—put on boots—read interpretation boards and the John Muir Trust's Schiehallion Path Appeal to Help repair the path to one of Scotland's most popular summits—follow clear track to summit of mountain, note glittering quartzite cone—take selfie on summit—identify neighbouring peaks and estimate distance to furthest—retrace steps to car park. Retire to pub.

Schiehallion was the first big hill the author climbed, and he sees more mileage in his describing that particular exploit and comparing it with another climb fifty years later than in giving a pedestrian guide-book account.

The summer of 1947 was the first after the war when bus tours ran again. Father and son had a week's tour of the Highlands and the son was particularly hooked on the far north-west, particularly on Suilven, the dramatic sugar loaf—the pillar-mountain of the Vikings. He decided that he would climb it the next year, but recognised that he would need to train.

Therefore, he would go off on his bike (on his own) for a week at Easter to Strathtummel Youth Hostel, near Pitlochry. This was not quite as negligent on the parents' part as it seems. The Pitlochry area was in a state of turmoil. The dynamic Secretary of State, Tom Johnston, was busily rejuvenating the Highlands and the area was buzzing as the Tummel-Garry Hydroelectric scheme was being engineered and every suitable hillside was being planted up by the Forestry Commission.

Achlean House had been taken over by the military during the war, and the main building was now leased by the Scottish Youth Hostels Association. The outbuildings—servant quarters, stables, etc.—were leased to the Forestry Commission as a hostel for their workers, among whom was the author's Uncle Bob. So the young author-to-be could have the freedom of travelling alone and looking after himself in the hostel, while uncle was available in the evenings for company and the resolution of any problems that might turn up.

From Edinburgh to Strathtummel was 77 miles and the author made an early start heading for the Queensferry Passage. The bike was a sturdy roadster fitted with a Sturmey Archer three-speed gear. The ferries could be very busy, with long queues, especially in summer, but these were no problem for the cyclist, who could just modestly slip aboard. Then it was off along the Perth road.

The cyclist sees much more than the motorist. Because he is slower and almost silent; he has time to observe and does not scare the wild life off. He also remembers much more detail of the journey, where every slight hill has to be fought up or freewheeled down.

So, after seventy years the thrushes' anvil on the roadside at Fordell is still remembered. Worse, as he cycled through every town and village, he remembers Cowdenbeath, which was, quite simply, hellish. Everywhere there was coal dust and soot, coal bings and mine railways.

Especially at the south end of the town were the monstrous effects of subsidence. Houses leaned at crazy angles and some were only kept upright by huge baulks of blackened timber.

The towns and villages like Kinross and Milnathort were better, gracious expressions of a kinder society. The run down Glenfarg was splendid. Downhill all the way, through a lovely winding glen, side by side with a railway that twisted and turned over the road. Bridge of Earn, the Earn itself, with a glimpse of the Highlands, and the view over Perth and the Tay were, as Para Handy says—'chust sublime'.

How wise the young lairds were, on returning from the Grand Tour, to build the little towers on Kinnoull and Moncrieffe Hills to remind them of the Rhine!

Beyond Perth, the presence of the Grampians ahead and to the left made itself felt and beyond Bankfoot, there was quite a stiff climb as the Highland Boundary Fault was crossed. The Tay was impressive, with a fine bridge at Dunkeld. Peaks were tipped with snow. For over 70 miles, he had been on the A90 and A9, but just beyond Pitlochry the main road was left, the Garry was crossed and the journey finished on B roads, which led, after 34 miles, to the remote Rannoch Station.

The last few miles to the hostel were impossibly hilly and no shame was felt at getting off the bike and pushing it uphill.

It was a good hostel and the young lad fitted in unobtrusively. The plan was to cycle around the old military roads and up some of the side glens, but an older chap in the common room persuaded him to climb Schiehallion the next day. It was a curious relationship. They very seldom spoke or even looked at each other.

The older chap had been at Paisley Grammar School, but when? He was older than the author, but by how much? Was his hair grey? The youngster never ever learnt his name.

In retrospect, the expedition the next day was not negligible. Indeed some might have called it over-ambitious. First, they had to cycle to the base of the hill. A few hundred yards (in 1948, metres in 1998) from the hostel/hotel, one comes to a highish point on the north side of Loch Tummel. This:

Had received the name of the 'Queen's View' some time prior to 3 Oct 1866, when the Queen first visited it, and here took tea. It commands a prospect of almost the entire basin of the river, from the mountains in the vicinity of Glencoe to those southward of Ben Vrackie—one of the grandest glen views in the United Kingdom.

10Km further on, we came to Tummel Bridge, where General Wade's road from Aberfeldy to Inverness crossed the Tummel, a wild and sizeable stream. Nearby was a large hydroelectric power station we considered an eyesore, especially as the hillside was degraded by the huge pipes bringing down the water. The author cannot recall whether they used Wade's bridge.

This seems unlikely as the power station was built in 1928 by the Grampian Electrical Company, and the construction work must have necessitated good access for heavy machinery, and a new bridge.

The next leg of the journey more or less followed the course of General Wade's Military Road to White Bridge, at 1000 feet, the highest point of the Aberfeldy road. This meant another 5Km and a climb of 200 metres.

The bikes were abandoned and they headed off westwards, up the slopes of Dun Coilich. The author was just wearing ordinary stout shoes and the heather persisted in undoing the laces. Unfortunately, the high start meant a dip and loss of height till the main climb up Schiehallion's west ridge was started. Now there was some snow to contend with, but not enough to conceal the masses of white quartzite at the top.

The author's first Ordnance Survey triangulation point was ritually touched and they took in the view. The details are forgotten but there remains a mental image of the great mass of the Carn Mairg massif to the south. Then came the descent and return, never as easy as one expects it to be—but freewheeling back to Tummel Bridge was a great reward!

It was a long time ago, but the author is sure that Uncle Bob must have been pleased with him, as they went together all round the north of Scotland in the summer, in rain and in shine!

At the end of the day, the bold climbers did not shout triumphally **Schiehallion! Schiehallion! Schiehallion!** But they must have been quite pleased with themselves.

And now, having come to the end of the stories about twelve Great Scots and their origins, we must ask whether there is a moral to these tales. The places vary and those I have classed as Great Scots vary enormously, but I suggest that one general conclusion is that, although Scotland may be just a small nation in the far north-west of Europe, on and below its tortured surface are beauty, romance and interest which have stimulated the growth and very being of great people.

Further Reading

Twelve Great Scots, scattered over Scotland, and indeed the world, with a variety of interesting characteristics, are bound to have generated a vast and diverse bibliography. Below is a selection from this. Most have been mentioned in the text and would be of benefit to anyone wishing to know more about what makes these places 'worth a detour', as the Michelin guides say.

Birkin, A. (1979) *JM Barrie and the Lost Boys*, New Haven and London: Yale University Press.

Bold, V., Nash, A. (eds) (2014) *Gateway to the Modern: Resituating JM Barrie,* Glasgow: Scottish Literature International.

Campbell, S. (2011) *Boswell's Bus Pass,* Dingwall: Sandstone Press.

Charlesworth, J. K. (1957) *The Quaternary Era*, London: Macmillan.

Dury, G. H. (1967) *Map Interpretation,* London: Pitman.

Hedderwick, M. (1992) *Highland Journey: A Sketching Tour of Scotland*, Edinburgh: Canongate.

Henderson, H. (1992) *Alias MacAlias: Writings on Songs, Folk and Literature,* Edinburgh: Polygon.

Lyell, C. (1997) *Principles of Geology*, London: Penguin Classics.

McKirdy, A., Gordon, J., Crofts, R. (2007) *Land of Mountain and Flood: The Geology and Landforms of Scotland*, Edinburgh: Birlinn Limited.

Martin, P. (2005) *Lochaber: A Historical Guide,* Edinburgh: Birlinn Limited.

Murray, D. (1883) *The York Buildings Company: A Chapter in Scottish History*, Glasgow: James Maclehose & Sons.

Noble, R. (2003) *North and West: Exploring the North and West Highlands and Islands of Scotland*, Dalkeith: Scottish Cultural Press.

Rider, M. (2005) *Hutton's Arse*, Rogart, Sutherland: Rider-French Consulting Ltd.

Robertson, J. (2013) *The Professor of Truth*, London: Hamish Hamilton.

Walker, C. K. (2002) *Breaking Away: Coleridge in Scotland*, New Haven & London: Yale University Press.

Williamson, A. G. (1946) *Twixt Forth and Clyde,* London: Putnam.

Illustrations – Plates

Plate 1a: Hutton's Unconformity – The Foundation of Evolution

Plate 1b: Allars Mill, Jedburgh

Plate 2a: Hutton's Section, Salisbury Crags, Edinburgh

Plate 2b: Scotland Special Sheet – Assynt

Plate 3a: Arkle, Inchnadamph

Plate 3b: De Hortus

Plate 4a: P & H, Amsterdam – Rhynia

Plate 4b: Rhynie, the Windyfield

Plate 5a: The Craw Stane, Rhynie

Plate 5b: Consumption dyke, Kingswells

Plate 6a: Barrie's Birthhouse – skeiner with thrums

Plate 6b: Barrie's grave – detail

Plate 7a: Inivie

Plate 7b: Dunblane Cathedral Memorial stone

Plate 8a: Dunblane – the golden pillar box

Plate 8b: Lockerbie – the memorial garden